# FAMINE TO FAIRYTALE

RUTH AND NAOMI'S PATH TO REDEMPTION

GENE & ELAINE GETZ

LifeWay | Small Groups

*Famine to Fairytale: Ruth and Naomi's Path to Redemption*
© 2006 Gene and Elaine Getz
Reprinted 2011

Published by Serendipity House Publishers
Nashville, Tennessee

All rights reserved. No part of this work may be reproduced, stored in a retrieval system, or transmitted in any form or by any means, electronic or mechanical, including photocopying and recording, without express written permission of the publisher. Requests for permission should be addressed to Serendipity House, One LifeWay Plaza, Nashville, TN 37234.

ISBN 978-1-5749-4230-9
Dewey Decimal Classification 248.843
Subject Headings:
CHRISTIAN LIFE \ WOMEN \ WOMEN IN THE BIBLE

Scripture quotations marked HCSB taken from the *Holman Christian Standard Bible*®, Copyright © 1999, 2000, 2002, 2003 by Holman Bible Publishers. Used by permission.

Scriptures marked NASB from the *New American Standard Bible*®, © 1960, 1962, 1963, 1968, 1971, 1972, 1973, 1975, 1977, 1995 by the Lockman Foundation. Used by permission.

Scriptures marked NIV taken from the *Holy Bible, New International Version*, Copyright © 1973, 1978, 1984 by International Bible Society. Used by permission.

Scriptures marked MSG taken from the *THE MESSAGE*, Copyright © 1993, 1994, 1995, 1996, 2000, 2001, 2002. Used by permission of NavPress Publishing Group.

Scriptures marked NLT taken from the *The Holy Bible, New Living Translation*, Copyright © 1996. Used by permission of Tyndale House Publishers, Inc. Wheaton, IL 60189, USA. All rights reserved.

To purchase additional copies of this resource or other studies:
ORDER ONLINE at www.SerendipityHouse.com;
WRITE Serendipity House, One LifeWay Plaza, Nashville, TN 37234
FAX (615) 251-5933 ~ PHONE (800) 458-2772

**SERENDIPITY HOUSE**

1-800-458-2772
www.SerendipityHouse.com

Printed in the United States of America

# Contents

Resource Credits ..... 4

Famine to Fairytale Introduction ..... 5

| Lesson | Title | Page |
|---|---|---|
| 1 | When Tragedy Strikes<br>Ruth 1:1-5 | 6 |
| 2 | Holding Onto Hope<br>Ruth 1:6-22 | 21 |
| 3 | Signs of Hope<br>Ruth 2:1-17 | 35 |
| 4 | Living Beyond Happiness<br>Ruth 2:18-23 | 50 |
| 5 | Going with a Different Dream<br>Ruth 3 | 63 |
| 6 | Happily Ever After<br>Ruth 4 | 77 |

## Leader's Guide

Required Session Supplies & Preparation ..... 91-93
Leading a Small Group ..... 94-96
Group Covenant ..... 97
Welcome to Community! ..... 98-101
About the Authors & Acknowledgments ..... 102
Meeting Planner ..... 103
Group Directory ..... 104

*Famine to Fairytale*

# HOME...WORKS
## MARRIAGE & FAMILY SERIES

Check these and other great studies
at www.SerendipityHouse.com ...

*Some Assembly Required: Instructions for an Amazing Marriage*

*Dream Team: The Power of Two*

*Turning Up the Heat: Rekindle Romance and Passion*

*Coauthoring Your Child's Story: Parenting on Purpose*

*Can You Hear Me Now?: Communication in Marriage*

*Creating Mutual Funds: Financial Teamwork in Marriage*

---

## CREDITS

Serendipity along with Gene and Elaine Getz wish to thank Regal Books, friends and partners in ministry, for graciously granting permission to include content from Gene and Elaine's book *The Measure of a Woman* in this Women of Purpose series.

# FAMINE TO FAIRYTALE

RUTH AND NAOMI'S PATH TO REDEMPTION

The Book of Ruth is an unforgettable love story between Ruth and Boaz, but the deeper parallel story is that of Ruth's—and especially Naomi's—redemption. Deeper still is the underlying message of the redemption God has for each one of us.

Both incredible women, the intertwined stories of Ruth and Naomi teach us so much about how God can bring incredible joy out of tragic circumstances. From the opening scene in the Book of Ruth, filled with famine and tragedy, to the almost fairytale ending, we see the real-life struggles. Real life is messy, and these women are far from perfect. Yet their faith and devotion through the pain and tragedy of life led each to experience unexpected joys and the blessings that God was longing to give them. In the same way, God has unexpected joys for each of us today!

*Famine to Fairytale* is a unique study for women, which blends fun elements, interactive discovery-focused Bible study, creative experiential activities, and wonderful opportunities to connect with God, with other women, and with your heart. Journal pages are provided with each session to support you in taking some of your deepest longings and questions to your heart and to God. Walk with Ruth and Naomi on their journey ...

- * When Tragedy Strikes – Coping with suffering and disappointment
- * Holding Onto Hope – Displaying honest emotion and pushing on
- * Signs of Hope – Taking our longings to God
- * Living Beyond Happiness – Allowing all things to drive us to God
- * Going with a Different Dream – Releasing lesser desires and dreams
- * Happily Ever After – Pursuing better dreams with joy

The Women of Purpose series highlights ordinary women used by God in extraordinary ways. As we delve below the surface and into the hearts of these women, we discover not only who they are, but also who *we* are. We find our hearts awakening to deeper intimacy with God and to an increasing desire to give ourselves to something grand, noble, and bigger than ourselves. We don't have to settle for simply existing; God created us to really live—to be women of passion and women of purpose.

# When Tragedy Strikes

The story of redemption is captured well in fairytales. Since girlhood, many of us have dreamed of living a fairytale. We long for adventure and the thrill of being claimed as royal brides. That yearning in our hearts is natural because we were created for a real-life fairytale. In fact, we're destined to find freedom from bondage through the King's love—a scenario not entirely unlike Cinderella's story.

Sadly, the original paradise God created for us is now lost for a time. When the Enemy deceived Adam and Eve and they rebelled against God's perfect plan, we became slaves to sin and struggle. But through Jesus we have a way out. Still, even after we come to faith in Jesus, we still must wait for the final "happily ever after" ending that God promises.

Real life is messy, and is at times filled with tragedy. Life's pain and heartaches seldom make sense to us, and can leave us wounded, discouraged, and disillusioned. As we walk the path of tragedy and triumph with Ruth and Naomi, let's consider how their story relates to our own.

## Breaking the Ice - *15-20 Minutes*

*LEADER: These "Breaking the Ice" questions and experiences are designed to get people talking. Spend a minute going around the circle as each woman introduces herself and shares one thing that she enjoys doing. Encourage each group member to respond to these questions so each one gets used to hearing her own voice in the discussions.*

1. Which of the following traveling styles best describes you or your life?

    ☒ First Class All The Way—I deserve it!
    ☒ I'll Take a Coach Seat—It's much more practical.
    ☒ Put Me on a Train—I'm pulling a long list of responsibilities.
    ☒ It's Time to Buy that Camper—I'm used to roughin' it.
    ☒ Set Me on a Cross-country Bike—I feel like my feet never stop pedaling.
    ☒ Picture Me on a Harley—I'm looking for adventure, Baby!
    ☒ Think Luxury Liner—It's about time for my ship to come in.
    ☒ I'd Backpack Up Mount Everest—I've got a ton of baggage and a mountain of "stuff" to conquer.
    ☒ Bring My Limo Around Front—I'm ready to be pampered.
    ☒ Other: _____.

*Session One*

*LEADER INSTRUCTIONS FOR THE GROUP EXPERIENCE: Be sure to bring a wide variety of PRECUT vacation-related pictures from travel brochures, vacation magazines, and newspapers. In advance, invite specific people to help with this. You'll also need small paper sacks (lunch bags) and glue sticks for each group member. Read together the instructions that follow, and allow group members about 5 minutes to create their paper bag collages.*

To get to know each other better, you'll each create a collage using the various vacation pictures provided by your leader. Using a small paper bag as your canvas, glue on pictures that detail the best trip you've ever taken on one side of the bag. Then, on the other side of the bag, glue pictures that represent your dream vacation. Lastly, put inside your bag one picture that symbolizes the souvenir you'd bring home from a dream vacation. After 5 minutes, your leader will gather the group together to present your bags.

2. **Show and Tell:** Using your bag to illustrate, briefly describe for the group the best trip you've ever taken. What made that experience so special? Describe your dream vacation. Why did you choose it?

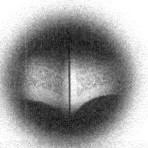

## DISCOVERING THE TRUTH
*20-25 Minutes*

*LEADER: In "Discovering the Truth," ask various group members to read the Bible passages aloud. Be sure to leave time for the "Embracing the Truth" and "Connecting" segments that follow this discussion.*

### DEFINITELY NOT A DREAM VACATION

We don't know much about Naomi's family or her husband Elimelech's, but Elimelech was likely from one of the prominent Jewish families of the day. He was the brother of Salmon, prince of Judah; he was a landowner; and the leaders of Bethlehem referred to him as "our brother" (Ruth 4:2-3). No doubt, Naomi began her married life in comfortable circumstances.

In spite of this promising start in life, the opening paragraphs of the Book of Ruth sound like a soap opera. Naomi and Elimelech felt compelled by circumstances to relocate, and their lives—once so full of promise— were never the same again.

*¹ During the time of the judges, there was a famine in the land. A man left Bethlehem in Judah with his wife and two sons to live in the land of Moab for a while. ² The man's name was Elimelech, and his wife's name was Naomi. The names of his two sons were Mahlon and Chilion. They were Ephrathites from Bethlehem in Judah. They entered the land of Moab and settled there. ³ Naomi's husband Elimelech died, and she was left with her two sons. ⁴ Her sons took Moabite women as their wives: one was named Orpah and the second was named Ruth. After they lived in Moab about 10 years, ⁵ both Mahlon and Chilion also died, and Naomi was left without her two children and without her husband.*

RUTH 1:1-5, HCSB

***LEADER:** Discuss as many discovery questions as time permits. Encourage participation by inviting different individuals to respond. It will help to highlight in advance the questions you don't want to miss. Be familiar with the Scripture Notes at the end of this session.*

1. Why did Elimelech and Naomi leave their home in Bethlehem? What length of visit and lifestyle plans do you think they might have made for their stay in Moab?

2. List the changes Naomi experienced in the 10 years summarized in Ruth 1:1-5. How do you think Naomi felt 10 years after arriving in Moab?

Naomi had moved from God's Promised Land in Judah to live among the Moabites. The Moabites were descended from Lot's eldest daughter through her incestuous relations with her father. Although the two races were generally related, they despised one another. The following passages offer clues as to why.

*¹ King Solomon was obsessed with women. Pharaoh's daughter was only the first of the many foreign women he loved—Moabite, Ammonite, Edomite, Sidonian, and Hittite. ² He took them from the surrounding pagan nations of which God had clearly warned Israel, "You must not marry them; they'll seduce you into infatuations with*

*Session One*

8

their gods." Solomon fell in love with them anyway, refusing to give them up. ³ He had seven hundred royal wives and three hundred concubines—a thousand women in all! And they did seduce him away from God. ⁴ As Solomon grew older, his wives beguiled him with their alien gods and he became unfaithful—he didn't stay true to his God as his father David had done. ⁵ Solomon took up with Ashtoreth, the whore goddess of the Sidonians, and Molech, the horrible god of the Ammonites.

⁶ Solomon openly defied God; he did not follow in his father David's footsteps. ⁷ He went on to build a sacred shrine to Chemosh, the horrible god of Moab, and to Molech, the horrible god of the Ammonites, on a hill just east of Jerusalem.

1 KINGS 11:1-7, THE MESSAGE

³ No Ammonite or Moabite may enter the LORD's assembly; none of their descendants, even to the tenth generation, may ever enter the LORD's assembly. ⁴ This is because they did not meet you with food and water on the journey after you came out of Egypt, and because Balaam son of Beor from Pethor in Aram-naharaim was hired to curse you.

DEUTERONOMY 23:3-4, HCSB

3. Why did God warn Israel about living closely with the pagan nations surrounding the Promised Land (1 Kings 11:1-2)? What reasons do you find for God's concerns about the Moabites in 1 Kings 11:4-6 and Deuteronomy 23:3-4?

4. What spiritual struggles might Naomi and her family members have experienced as a result of living in a pagan land with a people who worshiped "a horrible god," and who even resorted to lewd sexual practices and child sacrifices?

---

### *Principle for Living*
*For ourselves and for our families, we must take every precaution to avoid being seduced by the things of this world, which can and will draw us away from God.*

---

*Session One*

## THE BOTTOM DROPS OUT

In Hebrew, the word "Moab" means "waste," "emptiness," or "desolation." Elimelech had taken Naomi to Moab to escape difficulty and famine in Judah—to find a happier, more pleasant way of life. Life, however, doesn't always turn out the way we plan.

Naomi was in "Moab" in many ways. Along with her two daughters-in-law, she was on the brink of ruin—widowed, childless, impoverished, aging, desolate, and without wealth or property (which could be owned only by men). It wasn't enough that Naomi lost her husband and sons; she also lost her livelihood and dreams for the future.

*[Naomi spoke to Orpah and Ruth:] No, my daughters, my life is much too bitter for you to share, because the LORD's hand has turned against me.*
RUTH 1:13B, HCSB

5. What hopes and dreams for happiness were taken from Naomi? Why do you think God allowed such desolation to fill her life?

6. According to Ruth 1:13, what was Naomi's attitude toward God? How would you describe her feelings toward herself and life?

7. If you were in Naomi's situation, how would your faith in God be affected? What messages might keep playing in your mind?

Naomi was empty and desolate. She was in exile, and desperate. She viewed her life as "bitter," believing that the God she worshiped and loved had turned against her. Beyond her sorrow and feelings of abandonment, she may even have experienced guilt and shame. She was without any resources with which to improve her situation or to save herself from the brink of despair—she was forced to depend on someone else to redeem her.

> *Principle for Living*
> We cannot expect God to eliminate our suffering or even to decrease our hurts.
> It is not always God's goal to keep us happy or to make our dreams come true.
> For many, this creates a crisis of belief.

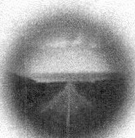

## EMBRACING THE TRUTH
*15-20 Minutes*

**LEADER:** *This section focuses on helping group members integrate what they've learned from the Bible into their own hearts and lives. Invite volunteers to read the Bible passages. Crabb's quote should resonate with group members who have been through difficult times. Set the tone for openness by sharing your own struggles with the group.*

### CRISIS OF FAITH

Author and counselor Larry Crabb sums up the dilemma that Noami and most of us face at some difficult point in our lives: "How are we to find hope when God's kindness hurts, when bad things happen that God could have prevented? ... We must discover a hope that thrives when dreams shatter, when sickness advances and poverty worsens and loneliness deepens and obscurity continues, the same hope that anchors us to God when dreams do come true." [1] In such instances, we must rely on these truths and promises from Scripture.

*I am the LORD, showing faithful love, justice, and righteousness on the earth, for I delight in these things. This is the LORD's declaration.*
                                                JEREMIAH 9:24B, HCSB

*God is faithful and He will not allow you to be tempted beyond what you are able, but with the temptation He will also provide a way of escape, so that you are able to bear it.*
                                                1 CORINTHIANS 10:13, HCSB

*[Solomon] said, "O LORD, the God of Israel, there is no God like You in heaven above or on earth beneath, keeping covenant and showing lovingkindness to Your servants who walk before You with all their heart."*
                                                1 KINGS 8:23, NASB

*Session One*

1. Faithfulness is a theme in each of these promises. According to these passages, what will God be faithful to do?

2. How can we reconcile God's faithful love, loving-kindness, and righteousness with Naomi's suffering? With the unjust pain and suffering in our own lives? In the lives of others around us?

3. Have you ever experienced a time when you felt separated from God because of hurts or difficult circumstances? As a group, brainstorm some thoughts and feelings that could affect people during times of pain.

The same uncertainties with which Naomi wrestled can keep us awake at night too. Every one of us must grapple with three vital questions when facing hurts, disappointments, and struggles.

(1) Can God really be trusted?
(2) Does God really have my best interests at heart?
(3) What is God trying to do in my life?

How we answer these questions determines whether or not we trust God enough to continue to follow Him.

*[Jesus invited:] ²⁸ "Come to Me, all who are weary and heavy-laden, and I will give you rest. ²⁹ Take My yoke upon you and learn from Me, for I am gentle and humble in heart, and you will find rest for your souls. ³⁰ For My yoke is easy and My burden is light."*

MATTHEW 11:28-30, NASB

4. What's Jesus' invitation for people who are worn out, overwhelmed, and weighed down? Will He prevent problems? What exactly does He offer?

5. Do you recall experiencing "rest for your soul" during a difficult time? Share your experience with the group.

---

*Principle for Living*

*Although He sometimes chooses to prevent or minimize pain in our lives, Jesus never promises to keep us from suffering. He does promise to walk with us through even the most awful situations, giving us genuine soul-rest.*

---

## CONNECTING *-10-15 Minutes*

**LEADER:** *Use "Connecting" as a time to begin to bond with, encourage, and support one another. Be accepting and invite everyone to join in the discussions. The goal of your "Connecting" time is to connect with one another, with God, and with your own heart.*

Naomi's life was in shambles—she was suffering, grieving, destitute, and feeling empty. It's important to recognize that pain and suffering are universal, but knowing that doesn't make our struggles any easier.

### THE BIG QUESTIONS WE ALL ASK

1. How have you heard well-meaning people try to spiritualize life's hardships and hurts? Why do you think so many people choose to superficially deal with pain or pretend everything is okay when it isn't?

2. To what things do people turn to escape pain and struggles?

3. In order to find out what God has for us in our suffering, we need to walk with Him through our pain until we find answers. What beliefs do we hold about God, life, and ourselves that keep us from staying in our pain and wrestling with God?

*LEADER INSTRUCTIONS FOR THE GROUP EXPERIENCE: Set up a CD player before your meeting and bring a copy of the CD album,* Behind the Eyes, *which contains Amy Grant and Wayne Kirkpatrick's song "Somewhere Down the Road." You could also download an MP3 version of the song from the Web.*

*Ask group members to close their eyes and think about the greatest challenges, struggles, or suffering they face as they listen to the song "Somewhere Down the Road." Using the CD is best, but if you're unable to obtain the CD for the meeting, at least read aloud the lyrics that follow. Discuss questions 4 and 5, review the Group Covenant, and then close your time in prayer and a quick review of "Taking It Home."*

Your current situation may not be nearly as difficult as Naomi's, but your journey through hardship is just as real. As you listen to the lyrics of this song, think about your greatest challenges and struggles. Allow God to speak to you through this song.

## SOMEWHERE DOWN THE ROAD

*So much pain and no good reason why*
*You've cried until the tears run dry*
*Nothing here can make you understand*
*The one thing that you held so dear*
*Is slipping from your hand*

*Session One*

*And you say,*
*Why, Why, Why? Does it go this way? Why, Why, Why? And all I can say is*

*Somewhere down the road*
*There'll be answers to your questions*
*Somewhere down the road*
*Though we cannot see it now*
*Somewhere down the road*
*You will find mighty arms reaching for you*
*And they will hold the answers at the end of the road.*[2]

4. What questions did you hear in this song that you have struggled with yourself?

5. As you listened to this song, what did you feel about what you're going through? Has God shared a message with you through either the song or in the story of Naomi and Ruth? If so, explain.

Those "mighty arms of a hero" sound appealing when circumstances come against us. Rescue from physical struggles, spiritual hunger, loneliness, and grief would certainly be a dream come true. But as the song says, the answers are "somewhere down the road." To take the journey, we must begin by trusting God despite our circumstances. In Session Two, we'll continue the difficult journey toward doing just that.

*LEADER: Take some time to go over the Group Covenant at the back of this book (page 97). Now is also the time for each person to pass around her book to collect contact information in the Group Directory on page 104.*

Share and record group prayer requests that you will regularly pray over between now and the next session. In addition to doing this, pray together that God will strengthen and encourage each participant as she takes her heart's deepest questions to God this week.

**PRAYER REQUESTS:**

# Taking It Home

*LEADER: Explain that the "Taking it Home" sections contain introspective questions as well as offering questions to take to God. Encourage each person to set aside quiet time this week so she can make the most of this study and group experience. Be sure to highlight the importance of writing down thoughts, feelings, and key insights that God reveals. Journaling is a powerful tool.*

Studying and discussing God's truth is not an end in itself. Our goal is always heart and life change. To take the next step of integrating the truth into our lives, we need to (1) look honestly into our hearts to understand the true motivations that drive us, and to (2) seek God's perspective on our lives. Psalm 51:6 says God "desires truth in the innermost being" (NASB).

## Questions to Take to My Heart

The following question asks you to look into your heart and focus on your deepest feelings about yourself. Our behaviors are the best indicators of what we really believe deep down. Look deep into the underlying beliefs in your heart where your truest attitudes and motives live. Spend some time in reflecting, and don't settle for a quick answer.

※ *When I go through difficult times and suffering, what does the way I respond indicate about what I believe about God? Do I feel that I can really trust Him? Does it seem He's really looking out for my best interests?*

*Session One*

# A Question to Take to God

When you ask God a question, expect His Spirit to guide your heart in His truth. Be careful not to rush or manufacture an answer. Don't write down what you think the "right answer" is. Don't turn the Bible into a reference book or spiritual encyclopedia. Just pose a question to God and wait on Him. Remember, the litmus test for anything we hear from God is alignment with the Bible as our ultimate source of truth. Keep a journal of the insights you gain from your times with God.

*God, sometimes You seem so far away. What do you think about the pain and struggles in my life? What do you want to say to me about trusting You through my pain?*

# Scripture Notes

## RUTH 1:1-5

*1:1 time of the judges.* These events happened after the Hebrews settled in the Promised Land, but before they received their first king, Saul. It was an unsettled and, at times, unsafe time in which "everyone did whatever he wanted" (Judges 17:6). *Bethlehem.* This is the same Bethlehem where Jesus was later born.

*1:3 Naomi's husband Elimelech died.* In these times a widow was destitute since women were often unable to work for a living and they were unable to own property. Naomi was even more at a disadvantage being a widow in a foreign land.

*1:4 Moabite.* The Moabites were descendants of Lot's son Moab (Gen. 19:30-36). Lot was Abraham's nephew. The people of Moab were pagans and represented everything that was detestable to the Jews. Marriage to Moabite women would have been clearly looked down upon by the people of Bethlehem.

*1:5 without her two children and without her husband.* Naomi was left alone, but in her culture that wasn't the worst of it. She was left with no one to carry on her family name and bloodline, which was of the utmost importance in that day and culture.

## 1 KINGS 8:23; 11:1-7

*8:23 no God like You in heaven above or on earth beneath.* Solomon acknowledged God's uniqueness and His faithfulness (see Ex. 9:14). This was an especially good reminder in view of the pagan deities of the surrounding Canaanites.

*11:1 many foreign women.* God forbade a king to marry many wives (see Deut. 17:17). He also forbade marrying foreign women because they worshiped false gods. Solomon, however, had 700 wives and 300 concubines. His pagan wives eventually led him into idolatry.

*11:4 they did seduce him away from God.* Solomon still believed in God, but he was drawn into disobedience and even worshiped other gods. He built high places east of Jerusalem for them.

*11:5 Ashtoreth.* A Canaanite goddess of sex, fertility, and war, whose worship involved sexual rites. *Molech.* Worship of this god (also called Milcom) included human sacrifices, especially children, which was strictly forbidden by God's law (see Lev. 18:21).

*11:6 Solomon openly defied God ... he did not follow his father David's footsteps.* David had remained true to God and had never worshiped false gods. David had always repented of his sin and returned to obedience. This is why God referred to him as "a man after God's own heart."

*Session One*

## DEUTERONOMY 23:3-4

*23:3 Moabite.* So how could David enter since he was the grandson of a Moabite woman (Ruth)? Some say that this prohibition was only for Moabite men. Others believe that the prohibition was only for the first 10 generations after the tabernacle was built.

## JEREMIAH 9:24

*9:24 boast ... that he understands and knows Me.* Everything of this world is temporary and not worth adoring. Boasting is risky, but if one is going to boast, let it be in knowing and understanding the eternal God. See also 1 Corinthians 1:31.

## 1 CORINTHIANS 10:13

*10:13 temptation.* Paul encourages the Corinthians to stand firm by reminding them that when Christians resist sin they do so in the knowledge that they will be able to endure temptation. Paul has identified various temptations that Israel faced: the temptation of idolatry, the temptation to commit sexual immorality, the temptation to test God, and the temptation to grumble about where God led them. To be tempted is to be tested. Facing the choice of deserting God's will or doing God's will, the person must either resist or yield. Temptation is not sin. Yielding is. *a way of escape.* Temptation is not unusual or unexpected. Resisting it is not pleasant, but the Christian can do it with God's help.

## MATTHEW 11:30

*11:30 burden.* The demands of discipleship, while costly in some ways (5-7; 8:18-22), are "light" in comparison with the demands of the Old Testament ceremonial law. Jesus promises to give us "rest for our souls" (v. 29) when we turn to Him in our struggles and desperation. Because of Jesus' grace, mercy, and delight in us, He persists in inviting us to His side so that He can care for us.

## SESSION QUOTATIONS

[1] Larry Crabb, *Shattered Dreams*, (Colorado Springs, CO: WaterBrook Press, 2001), p. 33.

[2] Lyrics from *http://lyrics.duble.com/lyrics/A/amy-grant-lyrics/amy-grant-somewhere-down-the-road-lyrics.htm* © by Amy Grant 1997.

# HOLDING ONTO HOPE

In the first session of *Famine to Fairytale*, Naomi and her two daughters-in-law were on the brink of ruin—widowed, childless, aging, desolate, and without property or wealth. Their dreams for the future were crushed. Through studying their situation, we explored the harsh reality that we cannot expect God to always minimize our pain, bring us happiness, or make our dreams come true. He does, however, want to walk with us and work with us in times of suffering.

In this session, we'll discover the paths Naomi, Orpah, and Ruth took after their lives fell apart. We'll walk with them in their pain, observe the strength of their characters, and discover how each held onto hope. Every woman in this group is dealing with a struggle; we each can learn a great deal from Ruth and Naomi's story. As a group, we have the wonderful opportunity to support one another as we find redemption in our pain through holding onto the hope of our Redeemer.

## BREAKING THE ICE - *15-20 Minutes*

*LEADER INSTRUCTIONS FOR THE GROUP EXPERIENCE: This craft experience is a fun way to introduce today's discussion. It should also help group members get to know each other better. Be sure to bring the following MATERIALS to your meeting: plain, inexpensive masks from a party or craft store; a variety of fun materials to decorate the masks (sequins, paints, feathers, lace, etc.); glue, colored markers, paint, and brushes. Allow only 10 minutes to create the masks so you have 5 minutes for "show and tell."*

Using the materials supplied by your leader, let your wild side out by creating a mask for yourself. You'll have no more than 10 minutes to create it before each person presents and explains her mask to the group. Don't aim for perfection; just have fun and let your personality shine.

1. **Show and Tell:** Take turns around the circle. Show your mask and briefly describe the reasoning behind your creation.

*Session Two*

21

2. Does your mask better represent who you really are or the person you'd like to be? Explain.

*LEADER: Encourage group members to share key insights from last session's "Taking It Home" questions. This should only take a couple of minutes, but allow a little extra time if someone has something inspiring to share. Affirm those who spent quiet time with God this week.*

3. How did your "Taking It Home" time go? What did you discover within your innermost beliefs about trusting God? Would you like to share with the group about what you heard from God about your own pain and struggles?

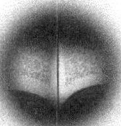

## DISCOVERING THE TRUTH
*20-25 Minutes*

*LEADER: In "Discovering the Truth," ask various group members to read the Bible passages aloud. Keep the discussion moving to allow time for the "Embracing the Truth," and "Connecting" segments that follow.*

### CHOOSING TO LEAVE MOAB

Often we avoid things that send us reeling into difficulty and stress, but we do get to choose how to respond to them. Naomi, Orpah, and Ruth faced a similar situation: they could stay trapped in desolation or emptiness (characterized by Moab) or they could leave to search for new life.

*⁶ When she heard in Moab that the LORD had come to the aid of His people by providing food for them, Naomi and her daughters-in-law prepared to return home from there. ⁷ With her two daughters-in-law she left the place where she had been living and set out on the road that would take them back to the land of Judah.*

RUTH 1:6-7, NIV

*LEADER: Discuss as many discovery questions as time permits. The strongest application questions appear in the "Embracing the Truth" section. Encourage participation by inviting different individuals to respond. It will help to highlight in advance the questions you don't want to miss. Be familiar with the "Scripture Notes" at the end of this session.*

1. According to verse 6, why did Naomi head back to Judah? What do you think she hoped to find upon returning to Bethlehem? What regrets do you expect she carried with her?

2. When Naomi and the young women chose to start moving on with life, were they immediately redeemed, made happy, and provided with new and better dreams? What did they have to gain from moving ahead with what little hope they still had?

## CHOOSING UNFAMILIAR PATHS

*⁸ [Naomi] said to them [Ruth and Orpah], "Each of you go back to your mother's home. May the LORD show faithful love to you as you have shown to the dead and to me. ⁹ May the LORD enable each of you to find security in the house of your new husband." She kissed them, and they wept loudly. ¹⁰ "No," they said to her. "We will go with you to your people."*
*¹¹ But Naomi replied, "Return home, my daughters. Why do you want to go with me? Am I able to have any more sons who could become your husbands? ¹² Return home, my daughters. Go on, for I am too old to have another husband. Even if I thought there was still hope for me to have a husband tonight and to bear sons, ¹³ would you be willing to wait for them to grow up? Would you restrain yourself from remarrying? No, my daughters, my life is much too bitter for you to share, because the LORD's hand has turned against me!"*
*¹⁴ Again they wept loudly, and Orpah kissed her mother-in-law, but Ruth clung to her.*

RUTH 1:8-14, HCSB

3. How do you imagine Orpah and Ruth felt about Naomi's insistence in verses 9-10 that they leave her and return home to remarry?

4. Both Orpah and Ruth loved Naomi, yet they responded differently to her urging. What does each woman's response indicate about her loyalty to Naomi and to her God? Why might Ruth have chosen to stick with Naomi in the midst of her own pain?

*Naomi* means "pleasantness" in Hebrew. True to her name, she carried a genuine concern for Orpah and Ruth She cared for them and recognized that life in Judah would be tough if they were not true God-followers.

Whether or not Naomi was intending to test the devotion and faith of her daughters-in-law, her request did just that. The name "Orpah" means "stiff-necked" or "stubborn." It's also said to mean "double-minded." Orpah was caught between loyalty to Naomi and life in Moab. "Ruth" on the other hand means "beauty to behold" or "friendship." Both names suit Ruth—a woman of beauty, strength of character, and unusual devotion.

> ### *Principle for Living*
> *Often in the midst of suffering or struggles, God sets a fork in the road. Your choices at these critical crossroads will set the course for your future.*

## CHOOSING GOD

*[15] Naomi said, "Look, your sister-in-law is going back to her people and her god. Follow your sister-in-law."*
*[16] But Ruth replied: "Do not persuade me to leave you or to go back and not follow you. For wherever you go, I will go, and wherever you live, I will live; your people will be my people, and your God will be my God. [17] Where you die I will die, and there I will be buried. May the LORD do this to me, and even more, if anything but death separates you and me." [18] When Naomi saw that Ruth was determined to go with her, she stopped trying to persuade her.*

RUTH 1:15-18, HCSB

5. What does Ruth's passionate reply in verses 16-17 indicate about her relationship with Naomi? About her relationship with God?

6. What kind of life might Naomi have lived to inspire Ruth's strong loyalty to her and to God? How can we live so that God is so real in our lives that others notice and are drawn to Him?

Because of the way Naomi lived, Ruth found the God of the Hebrews to be full of life, powerful, and worthy of following. Even in the midst of Naomi's struggles, God's light was able to shine through her to touch the heart of an unbeliever.

### *Principle for Living*
*Your life can send a powerful message of the amazing relationship a person can have with God. Even when you're spiritually and emotionally weak, God can use you to redeem the lives of those around you.*

## EMBRACING THE TRUTH
*15-20 Minutes*

**LEADER:** *This section focuses on the importance of grieving losses and unfulfilled dreams. To find God's redemption, we need to walk through our pain and be emotionally honest until we find His best for us. Keep this discussion practical and help group members integrate what they've learned from the Bible into their own hearts and lives. Invite volunteers to read the Bible passages aloud.*

## CHOOSING THE PATH THROUGH PAIN

*[19] So the two women went on until they came to Bethlehem. When they arrived in Bethlehem, the whole town was stirred because of them, and the women exclaimed, "Can this be Naomi?" [20] "Don't call me Naomi," she told them. "Call me Mara, because the Almighty has made my life very bitter. [21] I went away full, but the LORD has brought me back empty. Why call me Naomi? The LORD has afflicted me; the Almighty has brought misfortune upon me." [22] So Naomi returned from Moab accompanied by Ruth the Moabitess, her daughter-in-law, arriving in Bethlehem as the barley harvest was beginning.*

RUTH 1:19-22, NIV

Even after her 10-year absence, Naomi's return excited the entire town. She had clearly been well known and well liked. The women of Bethlehem were glad to welcome back one they remembered so fondly — this friend whose name means "pleasantness."

1. What do you think might have gone through Naomi's mind in verses 20-21? What similarities do you see between Naomi's outlook and that of others who fight despair?

2. Do you think Naomi's right about who she blames for the misery in her life (verses 20-21)? Why do you think God sometimes prevents suffering while allowing it at other times?

3. How do you imagine Naomi's friends and family initially reacted to her grief? How do people typically respond when someone continues to grieve and struggle over a long period of time?

Naomi was in despair, grieving her losses, unfulfilled dreams, and pain. To her, happiness seemed a faint memory never to be experienced again. That's why she changed her name from Naomi (pleasantness) to Mara (bitterness), letting everyone know her misery. Rather than hiding behind a mask of shallow spirituality, she admitted her depression and bitterness.

While it's likely everyone understood Naomi's grief for a short time, it's also likely that people quickly grew weary of it. We don't like to watch people grieving for long. In fact, we sometimes prefer everyone wearing a mask instead of being honest about their feelings. Larry Crabb warns against this attitude: "Church is too often a place of pretense and therefore a place without hope. When brokenness is disdained, where the real story is never told, the power of God is not felt. Where brokenness is invited and received with grace, the gospel comes alive with hope." [1]

*[16] Therefore we do not lose heart. Though outwardly we are wasting away, yet inwardly we are being renewed day by day. [17] For our light and momentary troubles are achieving for us an eternal glory that far outweighs them all. [18] So we fix our eyes not on what is seen, but on what is unseen. For what is seen is temporary, but what is unseen is eternal.*

2 CORINTHIANS 4:16-18, NIV

4. According to 2 Corinthians 4:16-18, how do we avoid losing heart in the midst of difficulties?

5. What's the larger perspective of suffering and redemption that God wants us to grasp (verses 17-18)?

6. Second Corinthians 4:16 shows that life can be a mess, but the mess itself is not God's primary concern. What greater purpose or dream could He want us to fight for and discover in our brokenness?

Session Two

> **Principle for Living**
> *To fulfill the deepest desires of your heart, you need to grieve honestly over your unfulfilled dreams. Fight through your pain and hold onto hope until you find everything God has for you on the other side of the pain.*

## CONNECTING - *10-15 Minutes*

***LEADER:*** *Use "Connecting" as a time to develop closeness within your group. Encourage and support one another. Invite everyone to join in; ask them to be open and honest with one another. Set the tone for openness: share your story first.*

Tears fell in the beginning of the story. Ruth and Naomi had plenty to cry about. It's likely that some from Bethlehem wept alongside them.

1. How does it feel when a friend comes to you in tears? What can you do to help in these situations?

2. How do you typically respond to losses or unfulfilled dreams in your life? When is grieving helpful and necessary?

### CHOOSING THE RIGHT PATH

***LEADER INSTRUCTIONS FOR THE GROUP EXPERIENCE:*** *If feasible, practice reading this Robert Frost poem aloud before group time. As a group, read through the introduction paragraph. Then ask group members to recall an important decision they have recently faced. Once they have decisions in mind, ask them to close their eyes and think about those decisions as you read aloud, "The Road Not Taken" by Robert Frost.*

*Session Two*

In the first chapter of Ruth, Naomi and her daughters-in-law make critical, life-altering decisions. Our lives are full of decisions, too. At each fork in the road we must make choices. Each choice can impact far more than we realize. The following poem by Robert Frost illustrates the emotional struggle we experience when forced to choose between paths. As your leader reads the poem, allow God to speak to your heart.

## THE ROAD NOT TAKEN

*Two roads diverged in a yellow wood,*
*And sorry I could not travel both*
*And be one traveler, long I stood*
*And looked down one as far as I could*
*To where it bent in the undergrowth;*

*Then took the other, as just as fair*
*And having perhaps the better claim,*
*Because it was grassy and wanted wear;*
*Though as for that, the passing there*
*Had worn them really about the same,*

*And both that morning equally lay*
*In leaves no step had trodden black*
*Oh, I kept the first for another day!*
*Yet knowing how way leads on to way,*
*I doubted if I should ever come back.*

*I shall be telling this with a sigh*
*Somewhere ages and ages hence:*
*two roads diverged in a wood, and I—*
*I took the one less traveled by,*
*And that has made all the difference.* [2]

3. Share insights that stood out to you from this poem. As you visualized your decision, did God show you the road "less traveled"? Explain.

*¹³ Enter through the narrow gate. For the gate is wide and the road is broad that leads to destruction, and there are many who go through it. ¹⁴ How narrow is the gate and difficult the road that leads to life, and few find it.*

MATTHEW 7:13-14, HCSB

4. According to Matthew 7:14, what's in store for those who take the road "less traveled"? In the past, what has helped you make wise decisions?

---

### *Principle for Living*
*In order to journey to redemption and life, you must choose the narrow road, the one others avoid or ignore. God's paths are often unfamiliar and difficult, but they lead to life.*

---

Share and record group prayer requests that you will regularly pray over between now and the next session. Also pray together today, asking God to open our hearts so we can share honestly with Him about our pains, struggles, doubts, and fears.

PRAYER REQUESTS:

# Taking It Home

*LEADER: For this week's "Taking it Home" activity, again encourage each person to set aside quiet time so she can make the most of this study and group experience. Be sure to highlight the importance of writing thoughts, feelings, and key insights God reveals in a journal. There's a fun and insightful exercise for each person to research the meaning of her name.*

## Project: What's in a Name?

In this session, we discussed the meaning and significance of names. Throughout Scripture, people attributed new names to God as they came to understand unique elements of His character. God also gave new names to people at significant times. Names of people and places have great significance in the Bible. In our culture, we don't always choose names based on their meaning, but names may still have significance.

As a fun exercise, research the meaning of your first name using a baby name book or better still Web sites such as: www.behindthename.com, www.zelo.com/firstnames, and www.babynamesworld.com.

## A Question to Take to My Heart

This question asks you to look into your heart and focus on your deepest feelings about yourself and your life. Look into your heart's underlying beliefs. Spend some time reflecting, and allow your feelings to surface.

❦ *What are some of my disappointments?*

Spend time taking these disappointments to God and grieve with Him over them. In many psalms, the writers and worshippers grieve and lament their losses and life situations. God can bring healing as we pour our hearts out to Him.

# A Question to Take to God

When you ask God a question, expect His Spirit to guide your heart in His truth. Be careful not to rush or manufacture an answer. Don't write down what you think the "right answer" is. Don't turn the Bible into a reference book or spiritual encyclopedia. Just pose a question to God and wait on Him. Remember, the litmus test for anything we hear from God is alignment with the Bible as our ultimate source of truth. Be sure to write down your disappointments and unfulfilled desires that surfaced in the question to your heart. Then, capture in writing what you hear from God.

⚜ *Almighty God and my Loving Father, how do You feel about my disappointments and unfulfilled dreams?*
*What would You like me to understand about this?*

# SCRIPTURE NOTES

## RUTH 1:6-22

*1:8 go back.* For several reasons Naomi would have seen the prospects for her daughters-in-law as bleak. Since she was widowed and alone, she could offer them few resources. Also, their prospects for marriage back in Bethlehem would be diminished since they were foreigners. *faithful love.* The particular brand of kindness described here speaks of God's grace and His loyalty to His covenant people, Israel. These women had been good to Naomi and her family. Now she was blessing them with the gracious kindness of God.

*1:11 Am I able to have any more sons?* According to the Law, when a woman was widowed, her deceased husband's closest relative (often a brother) would step in and care for her. This kept the family inheritance intact. As it stood, Naomi had no one else to offer these women to care for them. *your husbands.* In these ancient days an unmarried woman had no security. Naomi was doing the right thing for Orpah and Ruth to think first and foremost about their marital status.

*1:12 I am too old.* Naomi seems to feel that her options are completely depleted. A woman's role was to bear children, particularly sons. At one time Naomi had fulfilled that role, but now it had all been taken from her. A lifetime of effort was gone and she had nothing to show for it. She referred to this emptiness in verse 21.

*1:14 Ruth clung to her.* For all Ruth knew at that moment, she was giving up everything that mattered to a woman at that time in order to be loyal to Naomi. This supreme sacrifice on Ruth's part was rewarded in unexpected ways.

*1:15 god.* The chief god of Moab was Chemosh. At this point, it must have seemed to Naomi that there was more hope for her daughters-in-law in a culture of false worship than for three women alone traveling from Moab to Bethlehem. The other distinct possibility is that Naomi was trying to discern each one's true level of commitment to the Almighty God.

*1:16 I will go.* Ruth made an amazing commitment and sacrifice. She gave up her national identity, her religion, her home, and her own personal journey with no promise for any future or reward except to share in Naomi's sorrow.

*1:17 the LORD.* This amounted to a confession of faith for Ruth. She did not swear her loyalty according to her national gods, but to Naomi's God, Yahweh of Israel.

*1:20 Naomi.* This name means "sweetness" or "pleasantness." *Mara.* This name means "bitterness." During the Exodus, the Hebrews arrived at a place named "Marah," which was known for its bitter water (Ex. 15:23).

*Session Two*

*1:21 full ... empty.* The Book of Ruth is a story of Naomi's journey from a full life to an empty life and back to a full life again. *the Almighty has brought misfortune on me.* Still grieving, Naomi acknowledges that God is in control. Whether in good times or bad times, God is the Almighty One.

*1:22 arriving.* Naomi's return to her hometown is significant in several ways. She left in a famine and returned during a harvest (March or April). She returned with a famine in her spirit, yet she had Ruth with her, the one who would bring her such a great harvest of hope.

## MATTHEW 7:13-14

*7:13 gate is wide ... road is broad.* This is the way of the secular world that stands in contrast to the values taught in the Sermon on the Mount. *destruction.* This is where the "natural" way of the secular world leads. While ultimately such a lifestyle leads to the judgment of God against sin (Rom. 1:18), it also leads to destruction here and now in the sense of estranged relationships and inner chaos.

*7:14 narrow is the gate and difficult the road.* The narrower way is the way of life advocated by the Sermon. This way leads to an inner wholeness marked by the presence of God and fulfilling human relationships.

## SESSION QUOTATIONS

[1] Larry Crabb, *Shattered Dreams*, (Colorado Springs, CO: WaterBrook Press, 2001), p. 66.

[2] The American Academy of Poets Web site http://www.poets.org/viewmedia.php/prmMID/15717.

# SIGNS OF HOPE

In our last session, Orpah parted ways with Naomi after choosing to build her own life in Moab. Ruth, deeply devoted to Naomi and to Naomi's God, refused to leave her mother-in-law. Against this backdrop, we discussed the choices we face in difficult times. We learned that rather than giving up in despair, we need to choose to walk the unfamiliar paths of grief and loss like Naomi did. To allow God to fulfill the deepest desires of our hearts, we need to grieve honestly over our unfulfilled dreams and losses. Fighting through pain and holding onto hope are necessary steps in finding everything God has for us on the other side of the difficulties

In this session, we'll begin to see signs of hope as Naomi and Ruth courageously persevere. We'll see how God was at work in their lives both behind the scenes and in obvious ways. We'll see how God took these women under His wings, protecting and sustaining them—and we'll learn how He does the same for each of us.

## BREAKING THE ICE - *15-20 Minutes*

***LEADER INSTRUCTIONS FOR THE GROUP EXPERIENCE:****
This "Breaking the Ice" experience is designed to help people settle into the group setting and get them talking about the session topic. Before the meeting begins, set up a DVD player. Be sure to bring a DVD of the 2006 film* The Chronicles of Narnia: The Lion, The Witch and The Wardrobe, *created by Walt Disney Pictures and Walden Media. First read the introductory paragraph, and then show the movie scene.*

### WHO'S ASLAN?

In the movie version of C.S. Lewis' classic novel *The Lion, The Witch and the Wardrobe*, the world of Narnia has been devastated. Once peaceful and beautiful under the rule of the wise and magnificent lion Aslan, Narnia has now been turned into a land of fear and perpetual winter under the evil White Witch's reign. When four children stumble through an old wardrobe into Narnia's frozen landscape, their lives are never the same again.

*Session Three*

*LEADER: Show Scene 9 "Beavers' Home" (46:50 to 50:21 minutes on the DVD timer). After viewing the scene, discuss the following questions.*

1. What gave the beavers a sense that "there is hope" even in the midst of the desolation and losses in their lives?

2. Whom does Aslan represent in the real-life story of Naomi and Ruth? Share about a recent time in your life when you felt or knew that "Aslan was on the move."

3. How did the children respond to the prophecy about the bigger and better dream that Aslan planned for them? Why do you think they responded this way?

*LEADER: Encourage group members to share a key insight from last session's "Taking It Home" questions. This should only take a couple of minutes, but allow a little more time if someone has something inspiring to share. Affirm those who researched their names or spent time with their hearts and God, lamenting disappointments and unfulfilled desires.*

4. What did you discover about the meaning of your name? Do you think the meaning of your name fits who you are? Explain.

5. What did you hear from God about your disappointments, unfulfilled desires, or struggles?

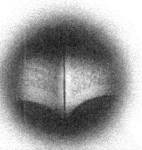

# Discovering the Truth
*30-35 Minutes*

*LEADER: In "Discovering the Truth," ask various group members to read the Bible passages aloud. Encourage each group member to share her unique perspectives on Ruth's story. This should be a lively discussion, but watch your agenda so you leave time for the "Embracing the Truth" and "Connecting" segments.*

## ASLAN'S ON THE MOVE

Entering Narnia brought all four of the children face-to-face with doubts, fears, and—later in the journey—excruciating pain and struggle. Given the choice, they would have escaped it all as quickly as possible, but they were stuck. The only option was to reluctantly press on down the unfamiliar path. As we pick up the story of Naomi and Ruth, we'll find they faced a similar situation ...

*1:22 They came to Bethlehem at the beginning of barley harvest. 2:1 Now Naomi had a kinsman of her husband, a man of great wealth, of the family of Elimelech, whose name was Boaz. 2 And Ruth the Moabitess said to Naomi, "Please let me go to the field and glean among the ears of grain after one in whose sight I may find favor." And she said to her, "Go, my daughter." 3 So she departed and went and gleaned in the field after the reapers; and she happened to come to the portion of the field belonging to Boaz, who was of the family of Elimelech.*

RUTH 1:22B; 2:1-3, NASB

*LEADER: Discuss as many discovery questions as time permits. Encourage participation by inviting different individuals to respond. Each one's perspective will be unique and enrich your discussions. It will help to highlight in advance the questions you don't want to miss. Be familiar with the "Scripture Notes" at the end of this session.*

1. As you read the story in Ruth 1:22 and 2:1-3, what do you see happening as a result of God working behind the scenes to protect and provide for Naomi and Ruth?

*Session Three*

2. To what signs of hope did Naomi cling in this dark time of her life? In question 1, we discussed God's role in her hope. What role did Ruth play in restoring hope?




God set up the practice of gleaning to ensure everybody willing to work was fed. This is one of the command God gave Moses on this topic:

⁹ *"When you harvest your crops, do not harvest the grain along the edges of your fields, and do not pick up what the harvesters drop.* ¹⁰ *It is the same with your grape crop—do not strip every last bunch of grapes from the vines, and do not pick up the grapes that fall to the ground. Leave them for the poor and the foreigners who live among you, for I, the LORD, am your God.*

LEVITICUS 19:9-10, NLT

3. For which people groups was God providing when He instructed landowners in Leviticus 19 about harvesting crops? What can we learn about Ruth as we see her willingly join the ranks of gleaners?




---

### *Principle for Living*
*As you refuse to retreat from life during trials, you accept by faith that God is still working in your life, even when His activity isn't visible. As you trust **who** God is and not **what** you see, you'll eventually see signs of hope that joy may return.*

---

## GOD'S HAND BECOMES VISIBLE

God, who's always working behind the scenes, orchestrated Naomi's return at the beginning of the harvest; He set up the practice of gleaning; He provided Elimelech's kinsman, Boaz, with great wealth and character; it was He who led Ruth to Boaz' fields. God's plan for Ruth and Naomi was becoming visible, but He had been at work longer than either imagined. Larry Crabb writes, "God is always working to make His children aware of a dream that lies beneath the rubble of every shattered dream, a new dream that when realized will release a new song sung with tears." [1]

⁴ *Just then Boaz arrived from Bethlehem and greeted the harvesters, "The LORD be with you!" "The LORD bless you!" they called back.*
⁵ *Boaz asked the foreman of his harvesters, "Whose young woman is that?"* ⁶ *The foreman replied, "She is the Moabitess who came back from Moab with Naomi.* ⁷ *She said, 'Please let me glean and gather among the sheaves behind the harvesters.' She went into the field and has worked steadily from morning till now, except for a short rest in the shelter."*
⁸ *So Boaz said to Ruth, "My daughter, listen to me. Don't go and glean in another field and don't go away from here. Stay here with my servant girls.* ⁹ *Watch the field where the men are harvesting, and follow along after the girls. I have told the men not to touch you. And whenever you are thirsty, go and get a drink from the water jars the men have filled."*

RUTH 2:4-9, NIV

Just after arriving to greet his harvesters and pitch in to work, Boaz noticed Ruth (verse 5).

4. What do you think so dramatically captured Boaz' attention from a distance? (Recall the meanings of Ruth's name and check Boaz' greeting in verse 8.) What character qualities were revealed about Ruth through the foreman's words (verses 6-7)?

5. Gleaning was difficult, demeaning, and dangerous work in Ruth's day. What special protection and provision did Boaz offer to Ruth?

---

### *Principle for Living*
*God uses life's adversities for your ultimate good. Both struggles and blessings are important elements in the larger story God wants to tell through your life.*

## GOD'S FAVOR

In Ruth 2:2, as she went out to glean the fields, Ruth hoped that she might find favor in the eyes of a Bethlehem landowners. As hoped, she did find favor in the eyes of Boaz. Two key reasons lay behind his kindness.

**LEADER: *Ask for three volunteers to read the parts of Ruth, Boaz, and the narrator.***

[NARRATOR] *¹⁰ Then she fell on her face, bowing to the ground and said to him,*

[RUTH] *"Why have I found favor in your sight that you should take notice of me, since I am a foreigner?"*

[BOAZ] *¹¹ "All that you have done for your mother-in-law after the death of your husband has been fully reported to me, and how you left your father and your mother and the land of your birth, and came to a people that you did not previously know.*

[BOAZ] *¹² "May the LORD reward your work, and your wages be full from the LORD, the God of Israel, under whose wings you have come to seek refuge."*

[RUTH] *¹³ "I have found favor in your sight, my lord, for you have comforted me and indeed have spoken kindly to your maidservant, though I am not like one of your maidservants."*

[BOAZ at MEALTIME] *¹⁴ "Come here, that you may eat of the bread and dip your piece of bread in the vinegar."*

[NARRATOR] *So she sat beside the reapers; and he served her roasted grain, and she ate and was satisfied and had some left. ¹⁵ When she rose to glean, Boaz commanded his servants, saying,*

[BOAZ] *"Let her glean even among the sheaves, and do not insult her. ¹⁶ "Also you shall purposely pull out for her some grain from the bundles and leave it that she may glean, and do not rebuke her."*

[NARRATOR] *¹⁷ So she gleaned in the field until evening. Then she beat out what she had gleaned, and it was about an ephah [more than half a bushel] of barley.*

RUTH 2:10-17, NASB

6. Boaz was the great grandson of Rahab, another foreigner who embraced the God of Israel. But even for a man of his background and character, his kindness and generosity to Ruth was unusual. According to verses 11-12, why did Ruth find such favor?

7. How would you describe Ruth's reputation in Bethlehem? What character traits may enabled Ruth to seek refuge under the "wings" of God (verse 13)?

8. In what other ways did Boaz shower kindness on Ruth? Do you think Boaz was so generous to Ruth only because he wanted to care for his relatives' widows, or was something more going on?

The name Boaz means, "In Him is strength" and the man's words to Ruth indicated that Boaz believed in and lived out that meaning. Both Boaz and Ruth were above reproach. Each carried a wonderful reputation in Bethlehem. Boaz had heard about Ruth before they met, but upon meeting her, he was immediately captivated. God's plan for redemption continues to unfold as the two begin to appreciate each other's good and loving qualities.

> ### Principle for Living
> God rewards people who follow Him through even difficult times in life. Boaz and Ruth reflected God's character and were rewarded. You too must have noble character in order to receive God's blessings and to encourage others to do the same way.

## EMBRACING THE TRUTH
*10-15 Minutes*

*LEADER: This section will help group members begin to look beyond their circumstances and emotions to focus on meeting the deepest needs and thirsts of their souls. Keep this discussion practical and help group members integrate what they've learned from the Bible into their own hearts and lives. Invite volunteers to read the Bible passages aloud.*

## OUR DEEPEST THIRSTS AND NEEDS

Naomi and Ruth were distressed and honest about their feelings, yet they persevered, living in search of God's best for them. There's nothing wrong with finding happiness in this life; God wants us to enjoy life. However, there is a problem when our goal is to find happiness by doing things on our own instead of seeking what God has in store for us.

*[God speaking in metaphor:] "For My people have committed a double evil: They have abandoned Me, the fountain of living water, and dug cisterns for themselves, cracked cisterns that cannot hold water."*

JEREMIAH 2:13, HCSB

1. What do the cisterns in Jeremiah 2:13 represent? What happens when we fall into the pattern of relying on our own resources rather than taking our deepest needs to God?

2. Why do you think we so easily abandon God, and try to create our own paths to happiness?

*¹³ Jesus said, "Everyone who drinks from this water will get thirsty again. ¹⁴ But whoever drinks from the water that I will give him will never get thirsty again—ever! In fact, the water I will give him will become a well of water springing up within him for eternal life."*

JOHN 4:13-14, HCSB

*³⁵ Jesus said, "I am the Bread of Life. The person who aligns with me hungers no more and thirsts no more, ever. ³⁶ I have told you this explicitly because even though you have seen me in action, you really don't believe me. ³⁷ Every person the Father gives me eventually comes running to me. And once that person is with me, I hold on and don't let go.*

JOHN 6:35-37, THE MESSAGE

3. What results does Jesus promise if we take our heart needs, disappointments, and hurts to Him? How does His offer differ from "digging our own cisterns" (Jeremiah 2:13)?

4. Jesus offers each of us a new life filled with truth, healing, and freedom from bitterness, despair, and our feeble attempts to find joy on our own. The catch is that we have to fight for it! In these verses from John, what does Jesus tell us we must do in order to receive this new life?

As each of us confronts life's ups and downs, we often turn to our "drugs of choice" that produce a sense of relief, comfort, release, or pleasure. To relieve the pain, we might take a drink, flirt a little, go shopping, dive into business success, eat, or just do whatever feels good This pattern, however, is a dangerous trap! To find freedom and life we must turn away from doing life our own way, turning instead to Jesus. He alone can heal our hurts and fill our hearts with the one thing we each search for and desperately need—an intimate relationship with Him.

> *Principle for Living*
> *To experience real joy and to embrace real life, you must realize that your deepest thirsts can be fulfilled only by Jesus, not through moments of pleasure or indulgence.*

## CONNECTING - *10-15 Minutes*

*LEADER: Use this "Connecting" time to deepen the sense of community within your group as you encourage and build up one another through whatever situations, big or small, each is now facing.*

Boaz expressed his confidence in God's ability to reward Ruth's faithfulness and to protect and care for her "under His wings." Ever our lover and protector, God invites each of us under His wings, too.

*¹ O God, listen to my cry! Hear my prayer! From the ends of the earth, I will cry to you for help, for my heart is overwhelmed. Lead me to the towering rock of safety, for you are my safe refuge, a fortress where my enemies cannot reach me. Let me live forever in your sanctuary, safe beneath the shelter of your wings!*

PSALM 61:1B-4, NLT

*Guard me as the apple of Your eye; hide me in the shadow of Your wings.*

PSALM 17:8, HCSB

*For You have been my help, and in the shadow of Your wings I sing for joy.*

PSALM 63:7, NASB

1. Which of these three Psalms best reflects your own experience? To which can you most relate? Explain.

2. All three of these psalms were written by David, a king well acquainted with trials, fear, and failure. Which of the truths in these psalms do you most need to be true in your own life?

3. Despite David's turmoil and fear, he always returned to the truth that he would find safety and joy in the shelter of God's wings. What does being in the shelter of God's wings mean to you?

Share and record group prayer requests that you will regularly pray over between now and the next session. Then pray together, asking that each participant will experience an overwhelming sense of God's presence and joy this week.

PRAYER REQUESTS:

## TAKING IT HOME

*LEADER: For this week's "Taking it Home" activity, invite each person in your group to identify a place in the area that's special to her to use for her quiet time with God. Perhaps there's a special mountain, river, garden, or building. For some, a bubble bath or sunroom will do the trick. Encourage the ladies to meet with God in that special place to ponder the questions for their hearts and for God.*

# A Question to Take to My Heart

This is introspection time—time to grapple with what drives your thinking and behavior, to understand what you really believe in your innermost being about God, yourself, and the world in which you live. Your behavior—not your intellectual stance—is the best indicator of your true beliefs.

- *To what or to whom have I really been turning for happiness and contentment? What keeps me from seeking shelter under God's wings, finding my heart's desire in Him?*

# A Question to Take to God

When you ask God a question, expect His Spirit to guide your heart in His truth. Be careful not to rush or manufacture an answer. Don't write down what you think the "right answer" is. Don't turn the Bible into a reference book or spiritual encyclopedia. Just pose a question to God and wait on Him. Remember, the litmus test for anything we hear from God is alignment with the Bible as our ultimate source of truth. Keep a journal of the insights you gain from your times with God.

*Am I really the apple of Your eye? How do You feel about me?*

# Scripture Notes

## RUTH 2:1-17

*2:1 relative.* The Law brought hope for a widowed woman, if a brother or other relative stepped in to carry on some of the deceased husband's responsibilities (Deut. 25:5-10).

*2:2 let me go.* Not simply tagging along, Ruth was taking responsibility for Naomi. It could have been dangerous for her to wander alone in the fields, yet that was the best way to get food. *fallen grain.* In Leviticus 19:9-10, the Hebrews were instructed to leave grain in their fields and grapes in their vineyards for the poor and widowed to glean from.

*2:3 She happened.* A typical expression that often denotes a story twist or coincidence, but in this case reveals the provision and providence of God, not mere coincidence.

*2:9 not to touch you.* This was a wonderful level of security for Ruth. With the kindness that Boaz showed her, she went from one lonely woman picking up grain amid strangers, to a woman among a group of women in a protected field. That was an amazing provision from God.

*2:11 your mother-in-law.* Evidently Naomi's story had spread throughout the town. Ruth's reputation of kindness toward Naomi was a good one. Boaz's description of Ruth's journey is reminiscent of his forefather Abram's journey described in Genesis 12:1.

*2:12 under whose wings.* Boaz used a beautiful image of protection to describe his hopes for Ruth. This same image is used by the psalmist in Psalm 91:4, 61:1-4, 17:8, 63:7 and by Jesus Himself in Matthew 23:37.

*2:13 my lord.* Ruth's character was revealed when she responded to Boaz with humility. She resists opportunism and responds with genuine gratitude.

*2:15 do not insult her.* The Law regarding gleaning required that the corners of a field and any dropped grain be left untouched for the gleaners. Some generous landowners left up to a fourth of their fields unharvested for the poor—a way of giving back to the community. Boaz went a step further. He asked his men to intentionally leave grain for Ruth.

*2:17 She beat out.* She beat the grain out from the stalks. *An ephah.* Half to 3/5 of a bushel—a large amount for one day of gleaning. This amount of grain from a single day's gleaning would feed Ruth and Naomi for 10 days.

## LEVITICUS 19:9-10

*19:9-10 what the harvesters drop.* This beautiful practice provided for the less fortunate. For instance, the widow Ruth met her future husband, Boaz, by gleaning in his fields (Ruth 2). A contemporary example is when restaurants send unused food to a homeless shelter.

JEREMIAH 2:13

*2:13 cracked cisterns.* Note the contrast between God and the pagan deities or our own efforts represented by idols. God was the source of life-sustaining water while the cisterns could not hold even a drop for the people to drink.

PSALMS 17:8; 61:1-4; 63:7

*61:2 ends of the earth.* The language is hyperbolic, but David nevertheless feels he is a great distance away from God—either physically (having fled from a threat; 42:6) or spiritually (facing death and sensing God's absence; 63:9). *towering rock of safety.* God is pictured as solid rock—an image first used by Moses (Deut. 32:4) and echoed elsewhere in the Psalms (62:2; 71:3; 91:1, 2; 144:1).

SESSION QUOTATIONS

[1] Larry Crabb, *Shattered Dreams*, (Colorado Springs, CO: WaterBrook Press, 2001), p. 82.

# LIVING BEYOND HAPPINESS

In Session Three, we began to see signs of hope as Ruth and Naomi courageously persevered in spite of their difficult circumstances. Both behind the scenes and in obvious ways, God was at work in their lives! He took the two women under His wings, protecting and sustaining them through Boaz. We, like Ruth and Naomi, must take our deepest thirsts to God. Rather than settling for temporary times of happiness, we can embrace real joy and real life by trusting God's plans for our lives.

In this session, Ruth returns from her first day in the fields and relays to Naomi the day's events. While Naomi's response may at first seem excessive, we should recognize that the news of Ruth shares becomes a true turning point for Naomi. It's at this point in the story that Naomi and Ruth learn to live beyond happiness, focusing instead on God's larger story of redemption.

*Session Four*

## BREAKING THE ICE  *10-15 Minutes*

*LEADER: The "Breaking the Ice" questions invite group members to share a part of their stories with each other and launch into the day's discussion. This should be light-hearted and should generate some laughs as you launch into your time together. For the sake of time, keep the demonstrations brief.*

1. Which of the following events would make you most happy? Why?
   - ☒ House fairies clean and organize my entire house
   - ☒ Aliens abduct my boss, so I'm now in charge
   - ☒ My children actually do what I ask without threats or bribes
   - ☒ The government sends me a $1,000 check by mistake and says to keep it
   - ☒ My weight loss program let's me eat real food, and it works
   - ☒ The man in my life hits his head and is transformed into Mr. Romance
   - ☒ Hershey's® names me the sweetest woman of the year and awards a year's supply of chocolate
   - ☒ A driver runs my children around all day while I relax at the spa
   - ☒ Other: _____

*LEADER DEMONSTRATION: Using a large bowl of water and a small dropper (e.g. a child's medicine dropper or syringe) discuss the "ripple effect" of events in our lives. Demonstrate that each drop sends ripples across the water's entire surface. Be sure to set up this demonstration before the meeting and test your technique. You need the right dropper, or the desired effect may not be produced. (Water can always be poured from a small pitcher if a dropper is not available.)*

2. Just as a drop in the bowl creates wave, events in our lives can have a ripple effect too. As a group, brainstorm events or actions that can have positive ripple effects in our lives and in the lives of others.

*LEADER DEMONSTRATION: This time, fill the dropper with food coloring. Carefully add the dropper-full of dye into the bowl. Show group members how a small amount quickly infuses the entire bowlful.*

3. When a situation seems huge and overwhelming, we must realize that events or perspectives can totally color our perception of the truth. How might you positively color your perceptions?

*LEADER: Encourage group members to share a key insight from "Taking It Home" questions. This should only take a couple of minutes, but allow a little more time if someone has something especially insightful to share. Affirm those who grappled with the topic of happiness this week.*

4. As you spent time searching your heart and talking to God about your relationship, what did you discover? Did you hear anything from God this week?

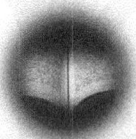

# Discovering the Truth
*25-30 Minutes*

**LEADER:** *Invite various group members to read the Bible passages aloud throughout this section. Your group should be gelling well now and enjoying good discussions. Encourage this, but watch your time. Be sure to leave time for the "Embracing the Truth" discussions and especially for the group experience in the "Connecting" time.*

## REIGNITING THE HEART

Only a few days had passed since Naomi returned to Bethlehem with the request, "Call me Mara, because the Almighty has made my life very bitter. I went away full, but the LORD has brought me back empty. … The LORD has afflicted me; the Almighty has brought misfortune upon me" (Ruth 1:20-21, NIV).

Naomi probably felt abandoned by God, perhaps wondering whether God even noticed her sorrow. In her first day in the fields, however, Ruth saw the Lord's hand at work. When Ruth returned home from gleaning, she reported the truth to Naomi: God had seen their plight and was actively meeting their needs.

> [18] *[Ruth] carried [the grain] back to town, and her mother-in-law saw how much she had gathered. Ruth also brought out and gave her what she had left over after she had eaten enough.* [19] *Her mother-in-law asked her, "Where did you glean today? Where did you work? Blessed be the man who took notice of you!"*
>
> RUTH 2:18-19A, NIV

**LEADER:** *Discuss as many discovery questions as time permits. This session will discuss the problem of pain and God's purposes in it. It will help to highlight in advance the questions you don't want to miss. Be familiar with the Scripture Notes at the end of this session to help clarify any issues.*

1. Given her bitterness and depression, Naomi's alertness to the unexpected blessings of God seems amazing. Given what you know about Naomi, why do you think she so quickly saw God's hand in the bounty Ruth brought home?

*Session Four*

2. How would you describe Naomi's emotional state after seeing what Ruth had gathered? What do think this event communicated to Naomi about God?

3. Why do you think Naomi continued to have faith in God despite her pain and struggles? To whom or what else might she have turned in her search for the life and joy she desired?

Naomi had been through a horrible 10-year ordeal. Although it had been a long time since she'd seen evidence of God's involvement in improving her situation, she quickly embraced God's activity when it came. Naomi was excited as she realized that God still truly cared for her and had not abandoned her.

> ### *Principle for Living*
> *Times of struggle or pain help you face your deep desire for connection and intimacy with God. God wants you to trust that His heart is good, cling to Him, and discover that all things—good and bad—point you to Him.*

## STILL MORE ...

[19] *Then Ruth told her mother-in-law about the one at whose place she had been working. "The name of the man I worked with today is Boaz," she said.* [20] *"The* LORD *bless him!" Naomi said to her daughter-in-law. "He has not stopped showing his kindness* [hesed] *to the living and the dead." She added, "That man is our close relative; he is one of our kinsman-redeemers."*

RUTH 2:19B-20, NIV

4. According to verse 20, why was Naomi pleased to hear the name of Ruth's benefactor?

*Hesed* is the Hebrew word translated "kindness" or "loving-kindness," though it may be best described as "faithful devotion." One of the central characteristics of God, *hesed*, is also often used in the context of marital love. Both cases refer to a covenant promise of endearing love and grace.

5. Read verse 20 again. Why do you think Naomi used the rich word *hesed* to describe Boaz' actions? What do you think Naomi meant by "He has not stopped showing his *hesed* to both the living and the dead"?

No doubt Naomi was seeing God's devotion to her and her entire family poured out through Boaz. Psalm 130 is one of many psalms about God's faithful *hesed* love. The psalmist refers to a difficult time in his life in which he traveled the same path that Naomi and Ruth took.

*¹ Out of the depths I call to You, LORD! ² Lord, listen to my voice; let Your ears be attentive to my cry for help. ³ LORD, if You considered sins, Lord, who could stand? ⁴ But with You there is forgiveness, so that You may be revered.*
*⁵ I wait for the LORD; I wait, and put my hope in His word. ⁶ I wait for the Lord more than watchmen for the morning—more than watchmen for the morning.*
*⁷ Israel, put your hope in the LORD. For there is faithful love* [hesed] *with the LORD, and with Him is redemption in abundance. ⁸ And He will redeem Israel from all its sins.*

PSALM 130, HCSB

6. What emotions are evident is the psalmist's words in verses 1-4? How do you think God responds to this depth of emotion and expression?

7. Describe the attitude with which the psalmist is waiting (verses 5-7). What sustains him even when he is crying "out of the depths"?

When life gets difficult, many people try to numb the pain or gloss over the hurts. Others give up on God altogether. Either path leads to settling for a superficial relationship with God. When Naomi's life in Moab unraveled before her eyes, she could have given up on God, choosing to go on in life without Him. She could also have avoided the hurt and settled for a superficial life with God. Instead, she embraced her pain, continued trusting God, and remained alert to His influence in her life. Because she experienced the depths of her heart, crying out to God and waiting for Him, Naomi met God in a new place of deeper intimacy and joy.

> ### *Principle for Living*
> *Allow yourself to experience the depths of your heart. Recognize that both happiness and suffering can lead you closer to God. Cling to God, and don't miss what He has for you in an attempt to gloss over or escape life's difficulties.*

## LIVING BEYOND HAPPINESS

Naomi was delighted to see God's active hand in her life again. Now that good things were happening, she could easily have focused on regaining the happiness she'd lost. Neither Ruth nor Naomi fell into the trap of selfishness or temporary happiness. Instead, they chose to focus on things better than just feeling good.

*²¹ Then Ruth the Moabitess said, "He even said to me, 'Stay with my workers until they finish harvesting all my grain.'" ²² Naomi said to Ruth her daughter-in-law, "It will be good for you, my daughter, to go with his girls, because in someone else's field you might be harmed." ²³ So Ruth stayed close to the servant girls of Boaz to glean until the barley and wheat harvests were finished. And she lived with her mother-in-law.*

RUTH 2:21-23, NIV

8. What do verses 21-23 highlight about the relationship between Ruth and Naomi? On what better things were these women focusing?

*Session Four*

# EMBRACING THE TRUTH
*10-15 Minutes*

**LEADER:** *This section focuses on helping group members begin to integrate what they've learned from Naomi's journey into their own lives. Discussions will highlight God's purposes in our lives during times of suffering. Invite volunteers to read the passages from Romans 8.*

## A MATTER OF PERSPECTIVE

*²⁶ In the same way the Spirit also helps our weakness; for we do not know how to pray as we should, but the Spirit Himself intercedes for us with groanings too deep for words; ²⁷ and He who searches the hearts knows what the mind of the Spirit is, because He intercedes for the saints according to the will of God. ²⁸ And we know that God causes all things to work together for good to those who love God, to those who are called according to His purpose.*

ROMANS 8:26-28, NASB

1. What promises in Romans 8:26-27 can help us when we feel too weak to make things right or even to cope with difficulties? How do these promises make you feel?

2. What does Romans 8:28 say that God "causes"? Does He cause the painful events in our lives? What does God do with these difficult situations?

*¹⁶ We are children of God, ¹⁷ and if children, heirs also, heirs of God and fellow heirs with Christ, if indeed we suffer with Him so that we may be glorified with Him. ¹⁸ For I consider that the sufferings of this present time are not worthy to be compared with the glory that is to be revealed to us. ¹⁹ For the anxious longing of all creation waits eagerly for the revealing of the sons of God.*

ROMANS 8:16-19, NASB

3. According to Romans 8:16-19, how does our suffering fit into the larger redemptive story? Which words in this passage tug at your heart? Explain.

4. What value is there in keeping the eternal vision and plan of God constantly before our eyes? What practical things can we do to keep our focus as "heirs of God" on the larger story?

### *Principle for Living*
*We are not yet in the final act of the larger story. Suffering and pain are part of our lives until God's Kingdom is fully established. When difficult times come, we must cling to God in our weakness, focusing on the eternal glory that awaits us.*

## CONNECTING  *15-20 Minutes*

*LEADER: Use "Connecting" as a time to deepen the sense of community within your group. The goal is to continue to deepen relationships with others in the group and to encourage one another through any difficult life situations. Invite everyone to join in, and set the tone for openness by sharing your story first.*

In *The Divine Embrace*, author Ken Gire discusses life as a dance with Jesus. To help us understand the value of difficult times in our lives, he explains the value of dissonance.

"We stumble not so much when the rhythms are pleasant and predictable as when they become grating and erratic. Whenever there is dissonance in music or in drama or in dancing, it is because certain rhythms need to be broken in order for new rhythms to be established. This is important to understand. Dissonance is about transition, and therefore it is a necessary part of the artistic whole."[1]

1. Has there been a time in your life when you've found dissonance to be a necessary part of your spiritual journey? Share with the group what you gained in the process.

2. Can you recall a rhythm or dream (even a small dream) that God has broken so you could learn and embrace a new one?

Nobody really likes discomfort, inconveniences, or difficulties, but God promises to use these things for our good (Romans 8:28). Your leader will guide you in a "listening prayer time" related to the struggles and dissonance in your life.

### *LEADER INSTRUCTIONS FOR A LISTENING PRAYER TIME:*
You're going to lead group members in a short time of listening prayer.

- Give each woman a washable, water-soluble fabric marker and a scrap of white cloth.
- Have a large bowl of water available.
- Allow this experience some time; don't rush it.
- Put on quiet background music (use the CD *Pursued by God: Redemptive Worship Volume 1* from Serendipity House, or select your own music); dim the lights if possible.
- Help each person create a small personal area. This is not a time to chat; make it very God-honoring.
- Trust God to speak to each person individually.

### *DIRECTIONS:*

(1) Ask your group members to close their eyes and envision their individual dance with Jesus, focusing on the grating, awkward, and erratic steps in that dance now.

(2) After a couple of minutes ask group members, "What roadblock, fear, or belief in your heart is preventing you from fully trusting God and clinging to Him tightly?"

(3) After a couple more minutes, say "When we choose to offer every part of our lives to God, even the most painful experiences can become beautiful acts of worship."

(4) Instruct group members to write their roadblocks, fears, or beliefs on the scrap piece of white cloth with washable fabric markers.

(5) Pray, asking God to release each woman from her roadblocks, fears, or wrong beliefs. Then ask each person to release her cloth into a bowl of water as an act of worship, and to symbolize committing it to God. NOTE: When water touches the marker, it will erase what is written.

3. Did God speak to your heart during the "listening prayer"? What do you think keeps you from finding all that God has for you in this time of life?

Share and record group prayer requests that you will regularly pray over between now and the next session. Close your time together with a prayer and a quick review of "Taking It Home" for this upcoming week.

**PRAYER REQUESTS:**

## TAKING IT HOME

*LEADER: This week's "Taking it Home" activity will focus on the dissonance in our lives, and the rhythms in our lives. Encourage each group member to find a quiet time this week to search her own heart and to take a question to God.*

## A QUESTION TO TAKE TO MY HEART

As you think about your own dance with Jesus, spend some time in introspection. Look into your heart and focus on your deepest desires and beliefs. Remember, our behaviors, not what we say we believe, are the best indicators of what we really believe deep down. Spend some time in reflecting on the uncomfortable, erratic steps in your dance with Jesus.

- *As I dance with Jesus, what missteps, erratic actions, and dissonance am I experiencing?*

*Session Four*

# A Question to Take to God

When you ask God a question, expect His Spirit to guide your heart in His truth. Be careful not to rush or manufacture an answer. Don't write down what you think the "right answer" is. Don't turn the Bible into a reference book or spiritual encyclopedia. Just pose a question to God and wait on Him. Remember, the litmus test for anything we hear from God is alignment with the Bible as our ultimate source of truth. Listen for a while and wait patiently for Him. Keep a journal of the insights you gain from your times with God.

❦ *Jesus, what rhythms are You trying to break in my life's dance? With what new rhythms or dreams are You trying to replace the old?*

SESSION QUOTATIONS

[1] Ken Gire, *The Divine Embrace*, (Wheaton, IL: Tyndale House Publishing, 2003), p. 125.

# SCRIPTURE NOTES

## RUTH 2:19-23

*2:19 Blessed.* Naomi immediately recognized that the large amount of grain must have been the result of special favor shown to Ruth.

*2:20 living and the dead.* Boaz showed kindness to the dead husbands of Ruth and Naomi by caring for their widows. *kinsman-redeemers.* According to Mosaic Law, a close relative had the privilege and responsibility to step in and provide for widows of his extended family. This could happen in a variety of ways, including through marriage or through the purchasing of property.

*2:23 until the ... harvests were finished.* During these few weeks the question still remained about how the women would fare after the harvest. The wheat harvest ended in late May-early June, so Ruth worked in Boaz' fields for a period of 4-6 weeks.

## PSALM 130

*130:1 I call to You.* This psalm of repentance may have been quoted during the Day of Atonement, the feast at which the Israelites confessed their sins (Lev. 16:29-30).

*130:4 there is forgiveness.* If God resolutely punished every sin and infraction of the law, no one would be left standing. The good news is that God forgives His people and blots out their sins.

*130:5-8 I wait.* God promises forgiveness for sins; that hope gives us faith to wait for God to act. It is God's unfailing love they have experienced in the past that gives them hope as they wait for His deliverance in the present. They know God doesn't give up on His people.

## ROMANS 8:16-19, 26-28

*8:16 The Spirit Himself testifies.* In the Roman adoptive proceedings there were witnesses to the ceremony who would, if a dispute arose, verify that the child had actually been adopted. The Holy Spirit is the One who verifies a person's adoption into God's family.

*8:17 heirs.* If someone is one of God's children, then that person is an heir, and will share in God's riches. In fact, Jesus is God's true heir (v. 3), but since believers are "in Christ," they become sons and daughters of God by adoption and thus are joint-heirs with Christ.

*8:18 sufferings of this present time.* The persecutions (5:3) that Christians face in the time between Jesus' first coming and His return. These are sufferings are real and unpleasant, but slight in comparison with the glory to lies ahead.

*8:26 how to pray.* It is not clear whether this refers to one's inability to know what to pray, or to the problem of knowing how to pray.

*8:28 God causes all things to work together.* God takes that which is adverse and painful (groans, persecution, even death—vv. 35-36) and brings profit out of it. *for good to those who love God.* This does not mean we preserve our comfort and convenience. Rather, God enables these difficult experiences to assist in our of salvation, growth, and redemption. *who are called according to His purpose.* The love people have for God is a reflection of the fact and reality of God's love for them expressed in His call to follow Jesus.

# GOING WITH A DIFFERENT DREAM

In Session Four, we discussed the favor Ruth received from a close relative or kinsman. When Boaz warmly responded to Ruth's presence in his fields, Naomi immediately recognized the hand of God at work in their lives. Her heart was reignited by confirmation that God had not abandoned her. As we left Ruth and Naomi in the last session, we concluded that suffering and pain are part of our lives until Jesus returns. That is why we must learn to allow all things, good and bad, to drive us closer to God.

In this session, Naomi still grieves her losses, but begins dreaming a new dream and establishing new life rhythms. As in the past, Naomi's faith spills over to ever-faithful Ruth, encouraging her to embrace God's plan. The lives of Ruth, Naomi, and Boaz become increasingly intertwined with God's larger story—taking some unexpected plot twists along the way.

## BREAKING THE ICE  *10-15 Minutes*

*LEADER: These "Breaking the Ice" questions invite group members to think about and share the stories of their lives. The goal is to start off on a lighter note, while engaging all group members in the interactions. Choose any or all of the questions that fit your group.*

1. You, too, are living out part of God's story. Which genre best matches your memoirs to date?

    ☒ Comedy—I'm having a ball!
    ☒ Drama—I guess that would make me a drama queen.
    ☒ Horror—Let me know when I can open my eyes.
    ☒ Slapstick—Life's a laugh a minute, with most jokes at my expense.
    ☒ Thriller—I find suspense waiting around every corner, like it or not.
    ☒ Fairytale—My story's complete with battles between good and evil, parables, and Prince Charming.
    ☒ Action-Adventure—My life has pretty well blown up, but I'm excited about the adventure ahead.
    ☒ Science Fiction—You don't want to know …
    ☒ Chick Flick—In the end I get everything I always dreamed of, but getting to the end is a major challenge.

*Session Five*

2. Keep in mind that your story is not yet finished. If you were writing the script, how would you like life to be different five years from now?

*LEADER: Encourage group members to share a key insight from last session's "Taking It Home" questions. This should only take a couple of minutes, but allow a little more time if someone has something inspiring to share. Affirm those who spent time alone with God.*

3. As you reflected on your dance with Jesus this week, what insights about old and new rhythms, and dissonance in your life did you discover in the questions to your heart or to God?

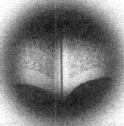

## Discovering the Truth
*20-25 Minutes*

*LEADER: Invite various group members to read the Bible passages aloud throughout this section. The focus today will be on Ruth and Naomi as women of excellence, Boaz as the model kinsman-redeemer, and the passion and restraint of our true Kinsman-Redeemer, Jesus Christ. Keep things moving at a steady pace through "Discovering the Truth" and "Embracing the Truth." Leave ample time for another group experience during the "Connecting" time.*

### FAMILY CARE

Ruth continued to work hard under the protection of Boaz until the end of the barley and wheat harvests. Although too old to work in the fields, Naomi was not idle. Her heart had been crushed by circumstances, but she patiently waited for God to move. When God's hand became evident to Naomi, her hope was reignited. Immediately she began moving ahead toward the new plan and hope that God had arranged.

*¹ One day Naomi her mother-in-law said to her, "My daughter, should I not try to find a home for you, where you will be well provided for? ² Is not Boaz, with whose servant girls you have been, a kinsman of ours? Tonight he will be winnowing barley on the threshing floor. ³ Wash and perfume yourself, and put on your best clothes. Then go down to the threshing floor, but don't let him know you are there until he has finished eating and drinking. ⁴ When he lies down, note the place where he is lying. Then go and uncover his feet and lie down. He will tell you what to do."*
*⁵ "I will do whatever you say," Ruth answered. ⁶ So she went down to the threshing floor and did everything her mother-in-law told her to do.*

RUTH 3:1-6, NIV

**LEADER:** *Discuss as many discovery questions as time permits. It will help to highlight in advance the questions you don't want to miss. Be familiar with the "Scripture Notes" at the end of this session to help clarify any issues.*

1. What do we learn in verses 1, 5, and 6 about Naomi's relationship with Ruth? Given the story so far and the character of these women, what do you think each woman's underlying motivation might have been in this interchange?

2. What do you think it was about Naomi that inspired Ruth to love and trust her? Why do you think Ruth agreed to follow Naomi's instructions?

*Session Five*

### Principle for Living
*In 1 Timothy 5:8 Paul explains that any one of us who doesn't provide for our relatives has "denied the faith and is worse than an unbeliever."*
*Caring for family members who are facing difficulties is right and honors God; but you should also extend this care into God's larger family.*

**65**

## FAMILY REDEEMER

In Ruth 2:20 and 3:1, Naomi unveiled her hope in Boaz as their "kinsman-redeemer," *goel* in the original Hebrew. According to John McArthur, the *goel* was "a relative who came to the rescue. The word *goel* includes the idea of redemption, or deliverance. ... A *goel* was usually a prominent male in one's extended family. He was the official guardian of the family's honor."[1] The *goel* might have a number of duties in his extended family, but two of these are central to Ruth and Naomi's story.

*²⁴ With every sale of land there must be a stipulation that the land can be redeemed at any time. ²⁵ If any of your Israelite relatives go bankrupt and are forced to sell some inherited land, then a close relative, a kinsman redeemer, may buy it back for them.*

LEVITICUS 25:24-25, NLT

*⁵ When brothers live on the same property and one of them dies without a son, the wife of the dead man may not marry a stranger outside the family. Her brother-in-law is to take her as his wife, have sexual relations with her, and perform the duty of a brother-in-law for her. ⁶ The first son she bears will carry on the name of the dead brother, so his name will not be blotted out from Israel.*

DEUTERONOMY 25:5-6, HCSB

3. In Old Testament times, women could neither own property nor carry on the family name. According to these two commands, in what ways was the kinsman-redeemer a rescuer?

4. What do the commands in Leviticus 25 and Deuteronomy 25 reveal to you about God's heart for people in hardships? How would you describe the heart of a true kinsman-redeemer (recall the meaning of *hesed* from Ruth 2:20)?

In Ruth's day, women were dependent upon the provision of men in their families. According to the Levirate Law mentioned in Leviticus and Deuteronomy, a widow might call on her nearest brother-in-law (*levir*) to perform a husband's duties, including provision of offspring and property. In cases like Ruth's in which there was no brother-in-law, the nearest of kin could be called on to act in the role of redeemer or *goel*. Each *goel* is a dramatic picture of the God who rescues and redeems each of us, buying back our lives from sin and destruction.

> ### *Principle for Living*
> *In times of hardship, as you wrestle with your unfulfilled desires, with your pain, and with God, you'll recognize that God is your Kinsman-Redeemer. He cares deeply. He alone is able to rescue you, fulfilling the deepest longings of your soul.*

## PURSUING THE REDEEMER

In Ruth 3:1-4, we saw Naomi's hope bloom as she began to pursue a new dream for her life.

5. Reread Ruth 3:1-4. What do you think Naomi had to release or give up in order to accept this new direction in her life and Ruth's? What risks do you see in the direction she chose?

To us Naomi's instructions to Ruth sound strange, even brash, but the steps Naomi laid out—while bold—were consistent with the customs. By following Naomi's advice, Ruth indicated her willingness to marry Boaz.

*⁷ When Boaz had finished eating and drinking and was in good spirits, he went over to lie down at the far end of the grain pile. Ruth approached quietly, uncovered his feet and lay down.*
*⁸ In the middle of the night something startled the man, and he turned and discovered a woman lying at his feet. ⁹ "Who are you?" he asked.*
*"I am your servant Ruth," she said. "Spread the corner of your garment over me, since you are a kinsman-redeemer."*

RUTH 3:7-9, NIV

6. What do you think Ruth's various motivations might have been in offering herself to Boaz in marriage? What feelings do you think she experienced in the hours leading up to this time?

> ### *Principle for Living*
> *You must release your lesser desires in order to pursue your Kinsman-Redeemer. As you relinquish control of your life's direction, you'll grow to trust in the sovereign God you can't control, as the source of real life.*

*¹⁰ [Boaz] said, "God bless you, my dear daughter! What a splendid expression of love! And when you could have had your pick of any of the young men around. ¹¹ And now, my dear daughter, don't you worry about a thing; I'll do all you could want or ask. Everybody in town knows what a courageous woman you are—a real prize! ¹² You're right, I am a close relative to you, but there is one even closer than I am. ¹³ So stay the rest of the night. In the morning, if he wants to exercise his customary rights and responsibilities as the closest covenant redeemer, he'll have his chance; but if he isn't interested, as God lives, I'll do it. Now go back to sleep until morning." ¹⁴ Ruth slept at his feet until dawn, but she got up while it was still dark and wouldn't be recognized. Then Boaz said to himself, "No one must know that Ruth came to the threshing floor." ¹⁵ So Boaz said, "Bring the shawl you're wearing and spread it out." She spread it out and he poured it full of barley, six measures, and put it on her shoulders. Then she went back to town.*

RUTH 3:10-15, THE MESSAGE

7. Why in verses 10-11 was Boaz so excited about Ruth's invitation? How does the rest of this scene portray the moral character of Ruth and Boaz?

> ### *Principle for Living*
> *The refreshing love story of Boaz and Ruth displays God's moral intentions for men and women. When you live with noble character and a commitment to morality, you reflect God's glory.*

8. Despite Boaz' attraction and admiration for Ruth, he held back from responding to her. Why? Why, according to verses 12-13, was the marriage invitation at risk?

## EMBRACING THE TRUTH
*10-15 Minutes*

*LEADER: This section focuses on helping group members begin to integrate into their own lives what we've learned from the Book of Ruth about abandoning our own desires and dreams so we can place our trust and hope in God alone. Discussions will highlight how God reveals His passion for us and why He doesn't seem to respond. Invite volunteers to read the Bible passages aloud.*

### AN UNRESPONSIVE REDEEMER?

Only months before her heart was touched by the relationship God was forming between Boaz and Ruth, Naomi was heartbroken, bitter, and on the verge of losing hope. But when she actually saw the hand of God moving and joined Him in what He was doing, Naomi became a new woman. She knew that Ruth was taken with Boaz, and believed that Boaz was taken with Ruth's youthful beauty and strength of character. But there was a problem. Ruth did not understand Jewish customs. When Boaz seemed to withdraw from Ruth's offer, the young woman must have been confused and troubled.

*[16] [Ruth] went to her mother-in-law, Naomi, who asked her, "How did it go, my daughter?" Then Ruth told her everything the man had done for her. [17] She said, "He gave me these six measures of barley, saying, 'Don't go back to your mother-in-law empty-handed.'"*
*[18] "Wait, my daughter," She said, "until you find out how things go, he won't rest unless he resolves this today."*

RUTH 3:16-18, HCSB

*Session Five*

1. How does Naomi respond to Ruth's confusion and worry (verse 18)? From Naomi's counsel and example, what can we learn when we feel like our Kinsman-Redeemer is not responding or is withdrawing from us?

2. Between Boaz' passionate response in verse 13 and Naomi's words in verse 18, we see a picture of this kinsman-redeemer's heart. If Boaz is a model of our Kinsman-Redeemer, what can we conclude about God's heart toward us?

3. Boaz had an important purpose in holding back from Ruth. Why do you think God, who is so passionate about us, sometimes holds back or delays in ending our difficulties and pain?

4. What do you think God might be trying to accomplish in our hearts by allowing us to struggle through disappointment and pain?

Author Larry Crabb makes this profound observation: "Because [God] longs to fill us, he hides His face long enough for us to discover how fervently and exclusively we want Him. ... Shattered dreams subject us to pain that weakens our stubborn grip on life as we want it and stirs our appetite for the thrill of God's presence. [2]

> *Principle for Living*
> When God seems distant or unresponsive, He may well be doing His most important and loving work in your life. He's your passionate Kinsman-Redeemer who "won't rest unless He resolves" things for your good. Wait with eager confidence and hope even in tough times.

## CONNECTING  *15-20 Minutes*

*LEADER: Use this "Connecting" time to deepen relationships within your group as you continue to help each other make sense of the journeys on which God is taking each of you. Encourage everyone to join in and to be open with one another. Set the tone by being transparent about your own struggles.*

*NOTE: Depending on the mood of the group, the end of this session might be a good time to discuss the idea of attending a conference together or planning a group retreat together.*

### GOING WITH A DIFFERENT DREAM

1. Each of us has desired things that are less than God desires for us. What are some lesser desires and dreams that sometimes capture more of your heart than God does? How has God revealed this to you?

*LEADER INSTRUCTIONS FOR THE GROUP EXPERIENCE:*
*Set up a DVD player before the session begins. Show Scenes 25, 26, and part of 27 from the film* Cheaper by the Dozen *(2003), which stars Steve Martin and Bonnie Hunt. Set the context for the scenes by reading the following paragraph. After viewing the movie scenes (1:26:50 to 1:30:53 on the DVD timer), discuss questions 2-4.*

In the 2003 film *Cheaper by the Dozen*, Tom (Steve Martin) and Kate (Bonnie Hunt) have 12 children and a busy home. Tom, who has been successfully coaching high school football for years, finally gets to live his dream—coaching at the college level. Tom and Kate move the family, wreaking havoc in the lives of all the children. Tom's dream job requires long hours away from his family, which brings more chaos. As Tom tries to pursue his dream and balance things at home, the college becomes unhappy with his work. He's asked to decide whether he's willing to give what it takes to fulfill his lifelong dream.

2. In the scene in which Tom's old friend and boss asks, "Giving up on the dream?" ... how do you feel about Tom's response? Explain.

3. With what internal conflicts and sacrifices did Tom have to struggle in making his decision? How do you think he felt about this?

4. When you look back on your life, what old dreams and life rhythms have you already traded for better dreams?

Share and record group prayer requests that you will regularly pray over between now and the next session. In addition to doing this, pray together that God will give each woman a sense of hope and of confident anticipation for Jesus, her Kinsman-Redeemer.

**PRAYER REQUESTS:**

# Taking It Home

*LEADER: "Taking it Home" this week allows group members to grapple with their own confidence in God and restraint of their Kinsman-Redeemer. Encourage each person to set aside quiet time this week so she can focus on her relationship with Jesus. Be sure to highlight the importance of writing down thoughts, feelings, and key insights that God reveals. Journaling is a powerful tool.*

## Trials & Blessings Chart

On a separate sheet of paper, create a column for "Trials" on the left side of the page and a column for "Blessings" on the left side. Jot down some hardships from your life in the Trials column, and list corresponding blessings that have emerged in the Blessings column. Not every of your past hardships will have obvious blessings yet.

## Questions to Take to My Heart

This is introspection time—time to grapple with what drives your thinking and behavior, to understand what you really believe in your innermost being about God, yourself, and the world in which you live. Your behavior—not your intellectual stance—is the best indicator of your true beliefs.

- *How easy is it for me to "wait" on God with hope and confidence when circumstances seem out of control?*
  *What do I believe in my innermost being about God or myself that causes me to doubt that my Kinsman-Redeemer will not rest until everything is resolved for my good (Ruth 3: 18)?*

*Session Five*

# A Question to Take to God

When you ask God a question, expect His Spirit to guide your heart in His truth. Be careful not to rush or manufacture an answer. Don't write down what you think the "right answer" is. Don't turn the Bible into a reference book or spiritual encyclopedia. Just pose a question to God and wait on Him. Remember, the litmus test for anything we hear from God is alignment with the Bible as our ultimate source of truth. Be sure to write down any insights you gain from your times with God.

*God, why do You seem so close at times and yet so far away and unresponsive at others? What do you want to say to me about the dreams I'm clutching?*

# Scripture Notes

RUTH 3:1-18

*3:1 should I not try to find a home for you.* Naomi's strategy toward helping Ruth had changed. Before they left Moab, Naomi urged Ruth to abandon her (1:8-12). Before as now, Naomi was seeking long-term security for Ruth. This time, Naomi wanted to help Ruth toward rescue and redemption, so she counseled the younger woman. Through her counsel, Naomi was able to return some of Ruth's care.

*3:2 winnowing.* Both threshing and winnowing were community events. Threshing was beating the grain from the stalks either with "flails" or by having oxen walk over the grain. Winnowing was throwing the grain into the air so that the wind would carry away the lighter chaff (like weeds) that had grown up with the grain. After winnowing, the grain was left in piles. Often a landowner (such as Boaz) would spend the night at the threshing floor to protect his product from theft.

*3:3 go down to the threshing floor.* This was a risky endeavor for Ruth. Women were not usually a part of the festivities. Some even think that Ruth's clothes were meant to disguise her until the men were sleeping. To follow Naomi's instructions in this way showed a lot of trust and courage on Ruth's part. Ruth was also risking that Boaz would reject her request for marriage.

*3:4 uncover his feet.* A request for marriage in that culture.

*3:5-6 I will do whatever you say.* Ruth followed Naomi's instructions because she was a godly, teachable woman and because she deeply respected and trusted Naomi. Naomi was a woman to be respected. She loved sacrificially; possessed wisdom, faith, and character; and inspired Ruth to love and trust her.

*3:9 Spread the corner of your garment over me.* Some translations render this "under your wing." The word used for "corner" also means "wings." Boaz's blessing to Ruth earlier had mentioned her being under God's wing (2:12). Now Ruth was asking to be under Boaz's wing as well.

*3:11 everyone in town.* Probably the elders of the town who often sat at the city gate dispensing wisdom and making judgments. *courageous woman.* This is often translated as "noble character." This comment is similar to the one made about Boaz (2:1).

*3:12 even closer than I am.* Here is an example of sophisticated ancient legal customs that involved inheritance and family structure. Boaz knew about a relative closer in bloodline to Ruth's husband than he was. Boaz had to deal with this legal matter before they could move ahead with any plan.

*3:13 stay the rest of the night.* Boaz protected Ruth by not sending her home in the middle of the night. *as God lives.* Boaz acknowledged faith in God as a part of his daily life and made a deep commitment to Ruth, even though he had to resolve the legal issues.

*Session Five*

*3:15-17 six measures.* Perhaps as much as 60 pounds of barley. *empty-handed.* Another beautiful image of God's provision for Naomi as He took her from her emptiness in Moab to her fullness in Bethlehem (1:21).

*3:18 he won't rest.* Naomi estimated Boaz well (4:1). Ruth had done what she could. The outcome now fell to Boaz, who would passionately pursue the matter on Ruth's behalf.

## LEVITICUS 25:24-25

*25:24 every sale of land.* This refers to the land someone has purchased. The original owners of the land are the tribesmen that the land was allotted to when the people of Israel returned home. Originally this referred to God's promise to Abraham and to the future division of the land among the tribes of Israel (Gen. 17:8, Josh. 13:6-7). *land can be redeemed.* The families that first received the allotment of the land will have the right to take possession again.

*25:25 a kinsman redeemer, may buy it back for them.* The land represented God's promise, His inheritance. It was a matter of concern for the whole tribe or extended family. That's why if someone sold the land due to financial difficulty, it was a relative's responsibility to step in and make sure the land remained in the family. In the Book of Ruth, Boaz was required to talk with the relative nearer to Ruth about his interest in purchasing the land for Ruth and Naomi (Ruth 4:1-10).

## DEUTERONOMY 25:5-10

*25:5-6* Survival of the family was essential to the governing of land, so these practices, which became foundational elements of the Israelite economy under Moses, were instituted to provide family heirs.

*25:9 remove his sandal.* This signifies a loss of rights in the Israelite community. *spit in his face.* A blatant act of contempt against the brother-in-law, indicating the seriousness of the charge.

## SESSION QUOTATIONS

[1] John McArthur, *Twelve Extraordinary Women*, (Nashville, TN: Nelson Books, 2005), p. 79.

[2] Larry Crabb, *Shattered Dreams*, (Colorado Springs, CO: Water-brook Press, 201), pp. 121, 129.

# HAPPILY EVER AFTER

As the story of Ruth and Naomi continued to unfold in Session Five, we saw Prince Charming, King Arthur, and the gallant white knight all captured in the character of Boaz, the swift and the strong. Boaz, as all genuine kinsman-redeemers, represents the ultimate Kinsman-Redeemer, Jesus Christ. Using the story of Ruth and Boaz, we discussed that only God can fulfill our deepest longings. In the midst of pain and difficulties, we can only heal and grow as we release our grip on lesser desires in order to wholeheartedly trust God with our hearts and lives.

Throughout five sessions of *Famine to Fairytale*, we've seen the famine, the "once upon a time," and plenty of ups and downs. Because fairytales mimic the great story of good and evil, suffering and redemption, paradise lost and paradise regained, they also have a "happily ever after." The Book of Ruth is not an idyllic fantasy, but a real-life reflection of the larger story of God's love and redemption ... with an incredible "happily ever after."

## BREAKING THE ICE  *10-15 Minutes*

*LEADER: These "Breaking the Ice" questions open the group dialog about our longings and hopeful anticipation. Keep this light-hearted.*

1. Which of the following story characters best describes your childhood approach to Christmas gifts?

   ☒ The Beast — People hid my gifts so I wouldn't rip them to shreds.
   ☒ Pandora — I couldn't help myself. I had to peek before Christmas.
   ☒ Shrek's Donkey — I drove my mother crazy as I asked at least daily if we could open something.
   ☒ Pinocchio — I didn't dare try anything; my nose would grow if I tried to lie or the little Jiminy Cricket in our house would tell on me.
   ☒ Scrooge — I just wasn't a big fan of all the holiday trappings.
   ☒ Goldilocks — I never opened gifts early, but I curiously shook and tried them all out one after the other.
   ☒ A clever little Hobbit — I tried to trick or bribe everyone into telling me what I was getting.
   ☒ Rumpelstiltskin — I loved to play the guessing game.
   ☒ Cinderella — I hated to spoil the surprise ... I wanted the celebration to be enchanting.
   ☒ Other: _____.

*Session Six*

2. As a young child, what things did you look forward to or long for at Christmas (or another favorite holiday)?

3. As an adult, what things do you now look forward to or long for at Christmas (or another favorite holiday)? What new longings have replaced your childhood longings from question 2?

4. As you spent time with your heart and God during this past week, what did you discover about your confidence, doubts, God's unresponsiveness, or your dreams?

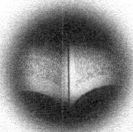

## DISCOVERING THE TRUTH
*25-30 Minutes*

*LEADER: Invite various group members to read the Bible passages aloud throughout this section. Be sure to leave ample time for the group experience and your study wrap-up during the "Connecting" time.*

### THE WAITING GAME

Waiting, longing, and hoping are a set of repeated themes in the Book of Ruth. Ruth and Naomi are at home awaiting the work of their kinsman-redeemer. And their kinsman-redeemer is waiting for the right opportunity to make his move. Boaz continues to demonstrate that he's a man of noble character as the story continues …

¹ *Meanwhile Boaz went up to the town gate and sat there. When the kinsman-redeemer he had mentioned came along, Boaz said, "Come over here, my friend, and sit down." So he went over and sat down.*
² *Boaz took ten of the elders of the town and said, "Sit here," and they did so.*
³ *Then he said to the kinsman-redeemer, "Naomi, who has come back from Moab, is selling the piece of land that belonged to our brother Elimelech.*
⁴ *I thought I should bring the matter to your attention and suggest that you buy it in the presence of these seated here and in the presence of the elders of my people. If you will redeem it, do so. But if you will not, tell me, so I will know. For no one has the right to do it except you, and I am next in line." "I will redeem it," he said.*

RUTH 4:1-4, NIV

**LEADER: *Discuss as many discovery questions as time permits. It will help to highlight in advance the questions you don't want to miss. Be familiar with the Scripture Notes at the end of this session to help clarify any issues.***

1. What do you think might have gone through Boaz' mind while he sat at the town gate waiting for his relative to pass by? What was the value in inviting the 10 elders to witness their discussion (verses 2, 4)?

2. With all of Elimelech and Naomi's sons and heirs dead, why was buying the land so appealing? What feelings do you imagine were stirred within Boaz when he heard the words, "I will redeem it"?

*Session Six*

### *Principle for Living*
*Men and women of noble character demonstrate respect and concern for the rights of others. As you live a life of integrity, others will be drawn to you and to the God you serve.*

## CLOSING THE DEAL

⁵ Then Boaz added, "You realize, don't you, that when you buy the field from Naomi, you also get Ruth the Moabite, the widow of our dead relative, along with the redeemer responsibility to have children with her to carry on the family inheritance."
⁶ Then the relative said, "Oh, I can't do that—I'd jeopardize my own family's inheritance. You go ahead and buy it—you can have my rights—I can't do it."
⁷ In the olden times in Israel, this is how they handled official business regarding matters of property and inheritance: a man would take off his shoe and give it to the other person. This was the same as an official seal or personal signature in Israel. ⁸ So when Boaz's "redeemer" relative said, "Go ahead and buy it," he signed the deal by pulling off his shoe.
⁹ Boaz then addressed the elders and all the people in the town square that day: "You are witnesses today that I have bought from Naomi everything that belonged to Elimelech and Kilion and Mahlon, ¹⁰ including responsibility for Ruth the foreigner, the widow of Mahlon—I'll take her as my wife and keep the name of the deceased alive along with his inheritance. The memory and reputation of the deceased is not going to disappear out of this family or from his hometown. To all this you are witnesses this very day."

RUTH 4:5-10, THE MESSAGE

3. Why did the kinsman-redeemer with first rights turn down the offer (verses 6-7)?




4. What was the difference between what Boaz and his relative were seeking to acquire? What was each one's motivation and what prize did each desire?




A true kinsman-redeemer will not act out of duty or personal gain, but out of deep affection and a desire to rescue, care for, and restore the person he will redeem.

> ### *Principle for Living*
> *Jesus, your Kinsman-Redeemer, has a profound affection for you.*
> *He counts it a privilege to rescue you, to redeem your life, and to lavish you*
> *with eternal riches and glory.*

## FINDING DEEP JOY

Although on the surface, the Book of Ruth is the story of Boaz and Ruth's romance, the deeper parallel story is that of Ruth's—and especially Naomi's—redemption. Author Larry Crabb suggests this central theme for the story:

> Shattered dreams open the door to better dreams, dreams that we do not properly value until the dreams that we improperly value are destroyed. Shattered dreams destroy false expectations, such as the "victorious" Christian life with no real struggle or failure. They help us discover true hope. We need the help of shattered dreams to put us in touch with what we most long for, to create an appetite for better dreams. And living for the better dreams generates a new, unfamiliar feeling that we eventually recognize as joy. [1]

> [13] *Boaz took Ruth and she became his wife. When he was intimate with her, the LORD enabled her to conceive, and she gave birth to a son.*
> [14] *Then the women said to Naomi, "Praise the LORD, who has not left you without a family redeemer today. May his name be famous in Israel.*
> [15] *He will renew your life and sustain you in your old age. Indeed, your daughter-in-law, who loves you and is better to you than seven sons, has given birth to him."*
> [16] *Naomi took the child, placed him on her lap, and took care of him.* [17] *The neighbor women said, "A son has been born to Naomi," and they named him Obed.*
>
> RUTH 4:13-17A, HCSB

5. Although Boaz was a wonderful kinsman-redeemer, he didn't receive the credit for the work of redemption in Naomi's life. Why do you think verses 13-14 credit God? Why is this significant to our lives?

6. What emotions do you imagine Naomi felt as she listened to the women and held her grandson on her lap (verses 14-17)?

7. Naomi allows friends to call her Naomi (pleasant) again rather than Mara (bitter). Her husband and sons are still dead. What seems to have changed in her life and heart to remove the bitterness?

8. Obed, the name the women of Bethlehem gave to Ruth and Boaz' son, means "a servant who worships." [2] How would you describe the evolution of Naomi's trust and worship over the course of her journey?

Obed's name (a servant who worships) expresses the end result of Naomi and Ruth's difficult journey. As Naomi holds her future in her lap, we see a beautiful expression of contentment and joy. Naomi, while still grieving losses and unfulfilled desires, has embraced her deepest desire for God and hope in Him alone. Through trials and blessings, God is telling the great story of redemption in and through our lives, too. Through glimpses of God's goodness, undistorted truth, and intimate connection with Him, our shallow faith, our shallow worship, and our shallow lives are being transformed by God.

> *Principle for Living*
> *The eternal joy and delight for which you were created is in the future, but you can hold the future in your lap today. As you abandon your life to God—as a worshiping servant, longing for intimacy—you can find hope, joy, and contentment that transcends circumstances.*

# EMBRACING THE TRUTH
*10-15 Minutes*

**LEADER:** *This section focuses on helping group members begin to integrate into their own lives what they've learned about God's redemption. Discussions will highlight glimpse of eternity that help us grasp our deepest desires and purpose.*

## TANTALIZING GLIMPSES OF ETERNITY

At the close of the Book of Ruth, a story much larger and greater than that of Ruth, Boaz, and Naomi is revealed. God went to great lengths to draw each of these three into His redemptive plan for the whole world.

Boaz was the son of Salmon (one of Joshua's spies at Jericho) and Rahab (the converted Canaanite prostitute who helped Israel conquer Jericho). Boaz became Ruth's kinsman-redeemer, and their marriage produced Obed, the grandfather of King David. It was the royal line of David that gave birth to Jesus, the Savior of the World.

*[17] [Obed] was the father of Jesse, the father of David. [18] Now this is the genealogy of Perez: Perez fathered Hezron. [19] Hezron fathered Ram, who fathered Amminadab. [20] Amminadab fathered Nahshon, who fathered Salmon. [21] Salmon fathered Boaz, who fathered Obed. [22] And Obed fathered Jesse, who fathered David.*

RUTH 4:17B-22, HCSB

1. With the perspective of the larger story revealed at the end of the Book of Ruth, what key events in the story now stand out to you as crucial?

2. Do you think Naomi or Ruth may have had a glimpse of God's plans for Obed? What can we learn from these women that will enable us to better play our parts in God's larger story?

*Session Six*

It's unlikely that Ruth and Naomi had any idea how important Obed and his legacy would be, but they both caught glimpses of God's heart and redemptive mission throughout their lives. C.S. Lewis explains how vital those glimpses into God's unseen reality are on our journeys:

> All things that have ever possessed your soul have been but hints of it—tantalizing glimpses, promises never quite fulfilled, echoes that died away just as they caught your ear. But if it should really become manifest—if there ever came an echo that did not die away but swelled into the sound itself—you would know it. Beyond all possibility of doubt you would say "Here at last is what I was made for." [3]

3. What are some tantalizing glimpses you've had of what you were "made for"? Briefly share one or two with the group.

We as God's future "bride" can embrace the promises that God makes to Israel in Isaiah 62. There He refers to Jesus' future reign when He comes back for His "bride" the church:

> [2] *The nations will see your righteousness, and all kings your glory; and you will be called by a new name which the mouth of the LORD will designate.* [3] *You will also be a crown of beauty in the hand of the LORD, and a royal diadem in the hand of your God.* [4] *It will no longer be said to you, "Forsaken," nor to your land will it any longer be said, "Desolate"; but you will be called, "My delight is in her," and your land, "Married"; for the LORD delights in you, and to Him your land will be married.* [5] *For as a young man marries a virgin, so your sons will marry you; and as the bridegroom rejoices over the bride, so your God will rejoice over you.*
>
> ISAIAH 62:2-5, NASB

4. According to Isaiah 62, how will life be different for us when Jesus comes back, binds the powers of evil, and fully establishes His Kingdom?

5. As you read these promises from God in Isaiah 62, what creates the deepest longing in your heart?

> ### *Principle for Living*
> *As you recognize your deepest desires through the ups and downs of life, you'll discover your longing above all else to know God deeply and personally, to please and enjoy Him, and to be a part of His redemptive mission to a hurting world (see Isaiah 61:1-3).*

## CONNECTING  *15-20 Minutes*

*LEADER: The discussion in this "Connecting" time will help group members open their hearts to the great romance and the Great Romancer.*

*NOTE: Before you close this final session of* Famine to Fairytale, *take a few minutes to discuss what your group will do next to continue the journey toward redemptive community. When will you meet? What will you study or discuss?*

### SAY IT AGAIN!

It seems only fitting to end the study *Famine to Fairytale* with a fairytale. *Ever After* (1998), which stars Drew Barrymore and Dougray Scott, is a contemporary retelling of the classic Cinderella story. Like the real-life story of Ruth, it's a rags to riches story of separation, hardship, passionate pursuit, rescue, redemption, oneness ... and of course "happily ever after."

*LEADER INSTRUCTIONS FOR THE GROUP EXPERIENCE: Have a TV/DVD player set up. Your final group experience will include two back-to-back scenes from* Ever After, *a contemporary retelling of the Cinderella fairytale. Show Scenes 26-27 (1:43:36 to 1:49:15 minutes on the DVD timer). Following the clip, discuss questions 1-4.*

1. What elements in this movie remind you of Ruth and Boaz? How about your love story with God? Explain.

2. In the end, Danielle is overwhelmed that a prince would so desire to marry a "commoner" or "peasant." How do you feel about the Lord's desire to embrace you as His eternal bride?

3. What did you feel when Danielle said, "Say it again ... The part where you said my name"? Why do you think those words gripped your heart? What do your feelings reveal about your deepest desires?

4. As you think back over the journey we've taken with Naomi and Ruth, what key changes have been effected in your beliefs and the way you approach life?

   Pray together for the journey of each woman in your group. Ask God to reveal, even this week, a tantalizing glimpse of what each one was made for in this life and for eternity.

   **PRAYER REQUESTS:**

# Taking It Home

*LEADER: "Taking it Home" this week focuses on experiencing God's joy and redemption. Encourage each person to set aside quiet time this week so she can make the most of this study and group experience. Be sure to highlight the importance of writing down thoughts, feelings, and key insights that God reveals.*

## A Question to Take to My Heart

This is introspection time—time to grapple with what drives your thinking and behavior, to understand what you really believe in your innermost being about God, yourself, and the world in which you live. Your behavior—not your intellectual stance—is the best indicator of your true beliefs.

❧ *How much true joy and contentment am I experiencing in my life? What beliefs about God, myself, or the world are keeping me from that joy? (Remember, joy is not temporary happiness, but a sustained sense of trust in and abandonment to God.)*

## QUESTIONS TO TAKE TO GOD

When you ask God a question, expect His Spirit to guide your heart in His truth. Be careful not to rush or manufacture an answer. Don't write down what you think the "right answer" is. Don't turn the Bible into a reference book or spiritual encyclopedia. Just pose a question to God and wait on Him. Remember, the litmus test for anything we hear from God is alignment with the Bible as our ultimate source of truth. Be sure to write down any insights you gain from your times with God.

⚜ *God, do I dare believe that you are my Kinsman-Redeemer? Are You really preparing a place just for me? Will You call my name just as the prince in the movie called Danielle's?*

# SCRIPTURE NOTES

## RUTH 4:1-22

*4:1 went up to the town gate.* The area around Jerusalem was hilly and the threshing floor was probably below the city. Boaz went to the city gate where business transactions took place. The kinsman-redeemer relationship involved something similar to a legal contract.

*4:2 ten of the elders of the town.* These men would function as witnesses of the transaction between Boaz and the nearer relative. No law stipulated 10 witnesses, but centuries later that number was required for a synagogue quorum, so it might have had traditional importance here.

*4:3 a piece of land.* Because the Hebrews' inheritance was the land God had promised them, each tribe and each family treasured their land. If Naomi's poverty caused her to sell the land, fellow tribesmen were obliged to buy it to keep it within the family.

*4:5 to carry on the family inheritance.* This was the heart of the law of the family redeemer. While the Law provided for the family to maintain their inheritance and for a widow to be cared for, the crux was that a man's legacy should not be taken away from him even in death. Ruth was honoring and maintaining Mahlon's (her dead husband, Naomi's son) legacy.

*4:6 jeopardize my own family's inheritance.* If Naomi had been the only widow involved, she would not have endangered this man's estate. She was past childbearing years. Ruth, on the other hand, could bear sons who would receive part of Ruth's estate, but also the family redeemer's estate after his death. Ruth's Moabite heritage may also have been a factor in his hesitation.

*4:9 bought from Naomi.* While Naomi was neither part of the proceedings nor the woman in question, ultimately her right to the land was being transferred.

*4:11 Rachel and Leah.* The 12 tribes of Israel descended from these two women, the wives of Jacob (who was later renamed "Israel" by God). The elders were blessing Boaz in mentioning these matriarchs.

*4:12 Perez.* An ancestor of Boaz, Perez was the product of a Levirate union. Tamar was first widowed by Er, and then eventually Judah (Er's father) took her in. She bore him twin sons, Perez and Zerah (Gen. 38).

*4:13-17 gave birth to a son.* At this point, Naomi had come full circle in her journey. She left Bethlehem with a family, then lost them all, and saved Ruth. But through God's provision, Naomi now held again the future—the inheritance of her husband and family.

*4:14 Naomi.* Even though the story of the Book of Ruth centers on the romance between Ruth and Boaz, the parallel story and conclusion focuses once again on God's provision for and redemption of Naomi.

*Session Six*

*4:15 better to you than seven sons.* The highest of praise from Hebrew women. Sons were considered of highest value. Seven sons symbolized all one could ever want (seven is often used to symbolize earthly perfection).

*4:16 placed him on her lap.* Joseph had done the same thing with his grandchildren as a symbol of ownership (Gen. 50:22-23), to indicate that they were as real to him as actual sons. At times this action even symbolized adoption.

*4:17 A son has been born to Naomi.* In the sense that Obed was Naomi's sole heir, this was a true statement.

*4:18-22 This genealogy stands as a reminder that God's plan reaches beyond generations.* From Naomi's sorrow came a grandchild who established the family line of both King David and then Jesus, the Messiah. Herbert Lockyer writes, "A Gentile by birth, Ruth yet became the chosen line through which later the Savior of the world appeared. As he came to redeem both Jew and Gentile alike, it was fitting that the blood of both should mingle in His veins."[4]

## ISAIAH 62:2-5

*62:1-5:* God is speaking in these verses to the nation of Israel about restoration during His millennial reign after His second coming. In general, these same promises apply to all Christ-followers.

*62:2 new name.* This signifies a new status and a new righteous character. Names in Scripture often represented one's anticipated or present character.

*62:4 "'My delight is in her."* A translation of "Hephzibah." *"Married."* A translation of "Beulah."

## SESSION QUOTATIONS

[1] Larry Crabb, *Shattered Dreams*, (Colorado Springs, CO: Waterbrook Press, 201), p. 35.

[2] Herbert Lockyer, *All the Women of the Bible*, (Grand Rapids, MI: Zondervan, 1967), p. 148.

[3] C.S. Lewis, *The Problem of Pain*, New York: McMillan, 1962), p. 146.

[4] Herbert Lockyer, *All the Women of the Bible*, (Grand Rapids, MI: Zondervan, 1967), p. 149.

# REQUIRED SUPPLIES AND PREPARATION FOR EACH SESSION

## SESSION 1:
### Dream Vacation Craft:

**Supplies:** - Variety of PRECUT vacation-related pictures from travel brochures, vacation magazines, and newspapers
- Small paper sacks (lunch bags) and glue sticks for each group member.

**Procedure:**
Instruct group members to create collages using the various vacation pictures. Using a small paper bag as a canvas, they will glue on pictures that detail the best trip they've ever taken on one side of the bag. Then, on the other side of the bag, they will glue pictures that represent a dream vacation. Lastly, they will put inside the bag one picture that symbolizes the souvenir they'd bring home from a dream vacation. After 5 minutes, gather the group together to present their bags.

### Somewhere Down the Road Music:

**Supplies:** - Set up a CD player before your meeting
- CD album, *Behind the Eyes*, which contains Amy Grant and Wayne Kirkpatrick's song "Somewhere Down the Road."
- You could also download an MP3 version from the Web

**Procedure:**
Ask group members to close their eyes and think about the greatest challenges, struggles, or suffering they face as they listen to the song "Somewhere Down the Road." If you're unable to obtain the CD for the meeting, ask at least read aloud the lyrics in the session.

## SESSION 2:
### Mask Creations:

**Supplies:** - Plain, inexpensive masks from a party or craft store
- Variety of fun materials to decorate the masks (sequins, paints, feathers, lace, etc.)
- Glue, colored markers, paint, and paint brushes

**Procedure:**
Allow only 10 minutes for group members to create masks for themselves. Gather the group for a quick 5-minute for "show and tell."

*Preparation*

### The Road Not Taken:

**Prep:** - Practice reading the Robert Frost poem aloud before group time.
**Procedure:**
As a group, read through the introduction paragraph. Then ask group members to recall an important decision they've recently faced. Once they have decisions in mind, ask them to close their eyes and think about those decisions as you read aloud, "The Road Not Taken" by Robert Frost.

### SESSION 3:

**What's in a Name?:** Research each member's name prior to the meeting

### Water Demonstration:

**Supplies:** - Large bowl of water
- Small dropper (e.g. a child's medicine dropper or syringe)
- Water can always be poured from a small pitcher if a dropper is not available
- Food coloring

**Procedure:**

DEMO #1 – Discuss the "ripple effect" of events in our lives. Add a drop from the dropper into the bowl. Demonstrate that each drop sends ripples across the water's entire surface. Be sure to set up this demonstration before the meeting and test your technique. You need the right dropper, or the desired effect may not be produced.

DEMO #2 – This time, fill the dropper with food coloring. Carefully add the dropper-full of dye into the bowl. Show group members how a small amount quickly infuses the entire bowlful.

### Listening Prayer Time:

**Supplies:** - Washable, water-soluble fabric marker and white cloth scrap for each group member
- A large bowl of water
- Quiet background music (*Pursued By God: Redemptive Worship* from Serendipity or your own music)

**Procedure:**
You'll lead the group in a guided listening prayer time. Allow this experience some time; don't rush it. Help each person create a small personal area. This is not a time to chat; make it very God-honoring. Trust God to speak to each person individually. Follow the 5 steps listed in this group experience at the end of Session Three.

SESSION 4:

**Supplies:** - Have a TV/DVD player set up
- *The Chronicles of Narnia: The Lion, The Witch and the Wardrobe* DVD (2006 by Walt Disney Pictures and Walden Media)

**Procedure:**
Read the introductory paragraph in the session, and then show Scene 9 "The Beavers." After viewing the movie scene (46:50 to 50:21 on the DVD timer), discuss questions 1-3.

SESSION 5:

**NOTE:** Depending on the mood of the group, the end of this session might be a good time to discuss the idea of attending a conference together or planning a group retreat together.

**Supplies:** - Have a TV/DVD player set up
- *Cheaper By the Dozen* DVD (2003 version with Steve Martin and Bonnie Hunt)

**Procedure:**
Show Scenes 25, 26, and part of 27 from the film *Cheaper by the Dozen*. Set the context for the scenes by reading the paragraph before question 2. After viewing the movie scenes (1:26:50 to 1:30:53 on the DVD timer), discuss questions 2-4.

SESSION 6:

**Supplies:** - Have a TV/DVD player set up
- *Ever After* DVD (1998 retelling of Cinderella with Drew Barrymore and Dougray Scott)

**Procedure:**
Your final group experience will include two back-to-back scenes from *Ever After*, a contemporary retelling of the Cinderella fairytale. Show Scenes 26-27 (1:43:36 to 1:49:15 minutes on the DVD timer). Following the clip, discuss questions 1-4.

*Preparation*

93

# Leading a Small Group

You will find a great deal of helpful information in this section that will be crucial for success as you lead your group.

Reading through this and utilizing the suggested principles and practices will greatly enhance the group experience. You need to accept the limitations of leadership. You cannot transform a life. You must lead your group to the Bible, the Holy Spirit, and the power of Christian community. By doing so your group will have all the tools necessary to draw closer to God and each other, and to experiencing heart transformation.

**Make the following things available at each session:**
- *Famine to Fairytale* book for each attendee
- Bible for each attendee
- Snacks and refreshments
- Pens or pencils for each attendee

### THE SETTING AND GENERAL TIPS:

1. Prepare for each meeting by reviewing the material, praying for each group member, asking the Holy Spirit to join you, and making Jesus the centerpiece of every experience.

2. Create the right environment by making sure chairs are arranged so each person can see the eyes of every other attendee. Set the room temperature at 69 degrees. If meeting in a home, make sure pets are in a location where they cannot interrupt the meeting. Request that cell phones are turned off unless someone is expecting an emergency call. Have music playing as people arrive (volume low enough for people to converse) and, if possible, burn a sweet-smelling candle.

3. Try to have soft drinks and coffee available for early arrivals.

4. Have someone with the spiritual gift of hospitality ready to make any new attendees feel welcome.

5. Be sure there is adequate lighting so that everyone can read without straining.

6. There are four types of questions used in each session: Observation (What is the passage telling us?), Interpretation (What does the passage mean?), Self-revelation (How am I doing in light of the truth

unveiled?), and Application (Now that I know what I know, what will I do to integrate this truth into my life?). You won't be able to use all the questions in each study, but be sure to use some from each.

7. Connect with group members away from group time. The amount of participation you have during your group meetings is directly related to the amount of time you connect with your group members away from the meeting time.

8. Don't get impatient about the depth of relationship group members are experiencing. Building real Christian Community takes time.

9. Be sure pens and/or pencils are available for attendees at each meeting.

10. Never ask someone to pray aloud without first getting their permission.

## LEADING MEETINGS:

1. Before the icebreakers, do not say, "Now we're going to do an icebreaker." The meeting should feel like a conversation from beginning to end, not a classroom experience.

2. Be certain every member responds to the icebreaker questions. The goal is for every person to hear his or her own voice early in the meeting. People will then feel comfortable to converse later on. If members can't think of a response, let them know you'll come back to them after the others have spoken.

3. Remember, a great group leader talks less than 10% of the time. If you ask a question and no one answers, just wait. If you create an environment where you fill the gaps of silence, the group will quickly learn they needn't join you in the conversation.

4. Don't be hesitant to call people by name as you ask them to respond to questions or to give their opinions. Be sensitive, but engage everyone in the conversation.

5. Don't ask people to read aloud unless you have gotten their permission prior to the meeting. Feel free to ask for volunteers to read.

6. Watch your time. If discussion time is extending past the time limits suggested, offer to the option of pressing on into other discussions or continuing the current session into your next meeting. REMEMBER: People and their needs are always more important than completing all the questions.

*Leading a Small Group*

## THE GROUP:

Each small group has it's own persona. Every group is made up of a unique set of personalities, backgrounds, and life experiences. This diversity creates a dynamic distinctive within a specific group of people. Embracing the unique character of your group and the individuals in that group is vital to group members experiencing all you're hoping to achieve.

Treat each person as special, responsible, and valuable members of this Christian community. By doing so you'll bring out the best in each of them, thus creating a living, breathing, life-changing group dynamic.

## YOU CAN HELP GROUP MEMBERS THROUGH ...

**Support** — Provide plenty of time for support among the group members. Encourage members to connect with each other between meetings when necessary.

**Shared Feelings** — Reassure the members that their feelings are very normal in a situation such as they are in. Encourage the members to share their feelings with one another.

**Advice Giving** — Avoid giving advice. Encourage cross-talk (members talking to each other), but limit advice giving. "Should" and "ought" statements tend to increase the guilt the loss has already created.

**Silence** — Silence is not a problem. Even though it may seem awkward, silence is just a sign that people are not ready to talk. It DOES NOT mean they aren't thinking or feeling. If the silence needs to be broken, be sure you break it with the desire to move forward.

**Prayer** — Prayer is vital to personal and community growth. Starting and ending with prayer is important. However, people may need prayer in the middle of the session. Here's a way to know when the time is right to pray. If a member is sharing and you sense a need to pray, then begin to look for a place to add it.

# Group Covenant

As you begin this study, it is important that your group covenant together, agreeing to live out important group values. Once these values are agreed upon, your group will be on its way to experiencing true Christian community. It's very important that your group discuss these values—preferably as you begin this study. The first session would be most appropriate.

- **Priority:** While we are in this group, we will give the group meetings priority.

- **Participation:** Everyone is encouraged to participate and no one dominates.

- **Respect:** Everyone is given the right to his or her own opinions, and all questions are encouraged and respected.

- **Confidentiality:** Anything that is said in our meetings is never repeated outside the meeting without permission.

- **Life Change:** We will regularly assess our progress toward applying the "steps" to an amazing marriage. We will complete the "Taking it Home" activities to reinforce what we are learning and better integrate those lessons into our lives.

- **Care and Support:** Permission is given to call upon each other at any time, especially in times of crisis. The group will provide care for every member.

- **Accountability:** We agree to let the members of our group hold us accountable to commitments we make in whatever loving ways we decide upon. Unsolicited advice giving is not permitted.

- **Empty Chair:** Our group will work together to fill the empty chair with an unchurched person or couple.

- **Mission:** We agree as a group to reach out and invite others to join us and to work toward multiplication of our group to form new groups.

- **Ministry:** We will encourage one another to volunteer to serve in a ministry and to support missions work by giving financially and/or personally serving.

I agree to all of the above_____ date: _____

# Welcome to Community!

Meeting together with a group of people to study God's Word and experience life together is an exciting adventure. A small group is ... *a group of people unwilling to settle for anything less than redemptive community.*

## Core Values

**Community:** God is relational, so He created us to live in relationship with Him and each other. Authentic community involves *sharing life together* and *connecting* on many levels with the people in our group.

**Group Process:** Developing authentic community requires a step-by-step process. It's a journey of sharing our stories with each other and learning together.

**Stages of Development:** Every healthy group goes through *various* stages as it matures over a period of months or years. We begin with the *birth* of a new group, deepen our relationships in the *growth* and *development* stages, and ultimately *multiply* to form other new groups.

**Interactive Bible Study:** God provided the Bible as an instruction manual of life. We need to deepen our understanding of God's Word. People learn and remember more as they wrestle with truth and learn from others. The process of Bible discovery and group interaction will enhance our growth.

**Experiential Growth:** The goal of studying the Bible together is not merely a quest for knowledge; this should result in real life change. Beyond solely reading, studying, and dissecting the Bible, being a disciple of Christ involves reunifying knowledge with experience. We do this by bringing our questions to God, opening a dialogue with our hearts (instead of killing our desires), and utilizing other ways to listen to God speak to us (group interaction, nature, art, movies, circumstances, etc.). Experiential growth is always grounded in the Bible as God's primary means of revelation and our ultimate truth-source.

**The Power of God:** Our processes and strategies will be ineffective unless we invite and embrace the presence and power of God. In order to experience community and growth, Jesus needs to be the centerpiece of our group experiences and the Holy Spirit must be at work.

**Redemptive Community:** Healing best happens within the context of community and in relationship. A key aspect of our spiritual development is seeing ourselves through the eyes of others, sharing our stories, and ultimately being set free from the secrets and the lies we embrace that enslave our souls.

**Mission:** God has invited us into a larger story with a great mission. It is a mission that involves setting captives free and healing the broken-hearted (Isaiah 61:1-2). However, we can only join in this mission to the degree that we've let Jesus bind up our wounds and set us free. As a group experiences true redemptive community, other people will be attracted to that group, and through that group to Jesus. We should be alert to inviting others while we maintain (and continue to fill) an "empty chair" in our meetings to remind us of others who need to encounter God and authentic Christian community.

## Stages of Group Life

Each healthy small group will move through various stages as it matures. There is no prescribed time frame for moving through these stages because each group is unique.

**Birth Stage:** This is the time in which group members form relationships and begin to develop community.

**Multiply Stage:** The group begins the multiplication process. Members pray about their involvement in establishing new groups. The new groups begin the cycle again with the Birth Stage.

**Growth Stage:** Here the group members begin to care for one another as they learn what it means to apply what they have discovered through Bible study, shared experiences, worship, and prayer.

**Develop Stage:** The Bible study and shared experiences deepen while the group members develop their gifts and skills. The group explores ways to invite neighbors, friends, and coworkers to meetings.

**Subgrouping:** If you have more than 12 people at a meeting, Serendipity recommends dividing into smaller subgroups after the "Breaking the Ice" segment. Ask one person to be the leader of each subgroup, following the "Leader" directions for the session. The Group Leader should bring the subgroups back together for the closing. Subgrouping is also very useful when more openness and intimacy is required. The "Connecting" segment in each session is a great time to divide into smaller groups of four to six people.

# Sharing Your Stories

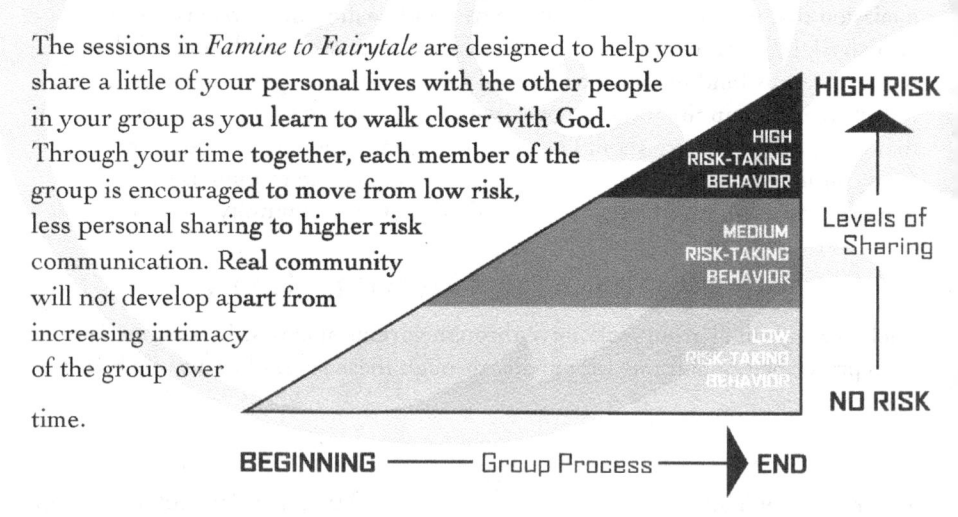

The sessions in *Famine to Fairytale* are designed to help you share a little of your **personal lives with the other people** in your group as **you learn to walk closer with God.** Through your time **together**, each member of the group is encourage**d to move from low risk,** less personal sharing **to higher risk** communication. **Real community** will not develop ap**art from** increasing intimacy of the group over time.

**HIGH RISK**
HIGH RISK-TAKING BEHAVIOR
MEDIUM RISK-TAKING BEHAVIOR
LOW RISK-TAKING BEHAVIOR
**NO RISK**

Levels of Sharing

**BEGINNING** ——— Group Process ——➤ **END**

# Sharing Your Lives

As you share your lives together during this time, it is important to recognize that it is God who has brought each person to this group, gifting the individuals to play a vital role in the group (1 Corinthians 12:1). Each of you was uniquely designed to contribute in your own unique way to building into the lives of the other people in your group. As you get to know one another better, consider the following four areas that will be unique for each person. These areas will help you get a "grip" on how you can better support others and how they can support you.

**G – Spiritual Gifts:** God has given you unique spiritual gifts (1 Corinthians 12; Romans 12:3-8; Ephesians 4:1-16; etc.).

**R – Resources:** You have resources that perhaps only you can share, including skill, abilities, possessions, money, and time (Acts 2:44-47; Ecclesiastes 4:9-12, etc.).

**I – Individual Experiences:** You have past experiences, both good and bad, that God can use to strengthen others (2 Corinthians 1:3-7; Romans 8:28, etc.).

**P – Passions:** There are things that excite and motivate you. God has given you those desires and passions to use for His purposes (Psalm 37:4,23; Proverbs 3:5-6,13-18; etc.).

To better understand how a group should function and develop in these four areas, consider going through the Serendipity study entitled *Great Beginnings*.

# GROUP MEETING STRUCTURE

Each of your group meetings will include a four-part agenda.

1. **Breaking the Ice:** This section includes fun, uplifting questions to warm up the group and help group members get to know one another better as they begin the journey of becoming a connected community. These questions prepare the group for meaningful discussion throughout the session.

2. **Discovering the Truth:** The heart of each session is the interactive Bible study time. The goal is for the group to discover biblical truths through open, discovery questions that lead to further investigation. The emphasis in this section is on understanding what the Bible says through interaction within your group.

   To help the group experience a greater sense of community, it is important for everybody to participate in the "Discovering the Truth" and "Embracing the Truth" discussions. Even though people in a group have differing levels of biblical knowledge, it is vital that group members encourage each other to share what they are observing, thinking, and feeling about the Bible passages. Scripture notes are provided at the end of each session to provide additional Bible understanding.

3. **Embracing the Truth:** All study should direct group members to action and life change. This section continues the Bible study time but with an emphasis on leading the group members toward integrating the truths they have discovered into their lives. The questions are very practical and application-focused.

4. **Connecting:** One of the key goals of this study is to lead group members to grow closer to one another as the group develops a sense of community. This section focuses on further application, as well as opportunities for encouraging, supporting, and praying for one another.

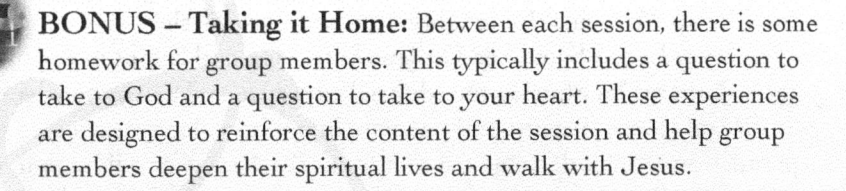

**BONUS – Taking it Home:** Between each session, there is some homework for group members. This typically includes a question to take to God and a question to take to your heart. These experiences are designed to reinforce the content of the session and help group members deepen their spiritual lives and walk with Jesus.

# About the Authors

More than 30,000 people currently attend Fellowship churches that Gene and Elaine Getz have planted in the Dallas area, while more churches span the globe. Dr. Gene Getz is a pastor, seminary professor, host of the "Renewal" radio program, and author of more than 50 books, including *The Walk*, *The Measure of a Man*, and *Building Up One Another*. Gene and Elaine recently released a revision of their best-selling book *The Measure of a Woman*. Elaine is a wonderful wife, mother, and grandmother, with much to pass on to younger women. The couple resides in Plano, Texas.

# Acknowledgments

We truly appreciate the effective partnership between my team at the Center for Church Renewal and the team at Serendipity, as well as all of the individuals who contributed to this effort.

We are deeply indebted to Iva Morelli and Sue Mitchell for their invaluable assistance in so many details of this and other projects.

My good friends at Serendipity have again done a wonderful job in every aspect of this Women of Purpose study. We especially want to thank …

- Publisher Ron Keck for his vision
- Ben Colter and Shauna Amick for working to develop this content into a small-group experience
- Brian Marschall for art direction and cover design
- Scott Lee of Scott Lee Designs for design and layout of the interior
- Bethany McShurley for editorial expertise and an eye for detail

Regal Books, friends and partners in ministry, have graciously granted permission to include some content from *The Measure of a Woman* in this Women of Purpose series.

# Meeting Planner

The leader or facilitator of our group is _____.
The apprentice facilitator for this group is _____.

## We will meet on the following dates and times:

|  | Date | Day | Time |
|---|---|---|---|
| Session 1 | _____ | _____ | _____ |
| Session 2 | _____ | _____ | _____ |
| Session 3 | _____ | _____ | _____ |
| Session 4 | _____ | _____ | _____ |
| Session 5 | _____ | _____ | _____ |
| Session 6 | _____ | _____ | _____ |

## We will meet at:

Session 1 _____
Session 2 _____
Session 3 _____
Session 4 _____
Session 5 _____
Session 6 _____

## Childcare will be arranged by:     Refreshments by:

| | Childcare | Refreshments |
|---|---|---|
| Session 1 | _____ | _____ |
| Session 2 | _____ | _____ |
| Session 3 | _____ | _____ |
| Session 4 | _____ | _____ |
| Session 5 | _____ | _____ |
| Session 6 | _____ | _____ |

# GROUP DIRECTORY

Write your name on this page. Pass your books around and ask your group members to fill in their names and contact information in each other's books.

Your Name: _____

Name: _____
Address: _____
City: _____
Zip Code: _____
Home Phone: _____
Mobile Phone: _____
E-mail: _____

Name: _____
Address: _____
City: _____
Zip Code: _____
Home Phone: _____
Mobile Phone: _____
E-mail: _____

Name: _____
Address: _____
City: _____
Zip Code: _____
Home Phone: _____
Mobile Phone: _____
E-mail: _____

Name: _____
Address: _____
City: _____
Zip Code: _____
Home Phone: _____
Mobile Phone: _____
E-mail: _____

Name: _____
Address: _____
City: _____
Zip Code: _____
Home Phone: _____
Mobile Phone: _____
E-mail: _____

Name: _____
Address: _____
City: _____
Zip Code: _____
Home Phone: _____
Mobile Phone: _____
E-mail: _____

Name: _____
Address: _____
City: _____
Zip Code: _____
Home Phone: _____
Mobile Phone: _____
E-mail: _____

Name: _____
Address: _____
City: _____
Zip Code: _____
Home Phone: _____
Mobile Phone: _____
E-mail: _____

Name: _____
Address: _____
City: _____
Zip Code: _____
Home Phone: _____
Mobile Phone: _____
E-mail: _____

Name: _____
Address: _____
City: _____
Zip Code: _____
Home Phone: _____
Mobile Phone: _____
E-mail: _____

Name: _____
Address: _____
City: _____
Zip Code: _____
Home Phone: _____
Mobile Phone: _____
E-mail: _____

Name: _____
Address: _____
City: _____
Zip Code: _____
Home Phone: _____
Mobile Phone: _____
E-mail: _____